The Financial Reporting

Project and Readings

3e

Bruce A. Baldwin
Arizona State University West

Clayton A. Hock
Miami University

SOUTH-WESTERN

THOMSON LEARNING

Australia · Canada · Mexico · Singapore · Spain · United Kingdom · United States

The Financial Reporting Project And Readings for Learning Teams or Individuals, 3e by
Bruce A. Baldwin and Clayton A. Hock

Team Director: Melissa Acuna
Senior Acquisitions Editor: Sharon Oblinger
Senior Developmental Editor: Sara E. Wilson
Production Editor: Amy McGuire
Media Production Editor: Lora Craver
Marketing Manager: Larry Qualls
Manufacturing Coordinator: Doug Wilke
Printer: Globus Printing, Inc.

Printed in the United States of America
1 2 3 4 5 05 04 03 02 01

For more information contact South-Western, 5101 Madison Road, Cincinnati, Ohio,
45227 or find us on the Internet at http://www.swcollege.com

For permission to use material from this text or product, contact us by
- **Telephone: 1-800-730-2214**
- **Fax: 1-800-730-2215**
- **Web: http://www.thomsonrights.com**

ISBN: 0-324-12580-1

Preface to the Student

The primary purpose of the **Financial Reporting Project (FRP)** is for you to experience up-to-date *live* financial statements *in their natural habitat*. For most users of financial statements, the natural habitat is the Annual Report to Stockholders or the Securities and Exchange Commission (SEC) Form 10-K Report. While portions of real financial statements are illustrated in the textbook, this project will *put it all together*. You will work with the complete and integrated financial reports of a live company as you apply the lessons of your accounting course. The development and application of this accounting knowledge will advance your career.

Be aware that, occasionally, some of the ratio formulas you use in this project are slightly different from the basic ratio formulas used in the text. This is necessary because of the more complex data you will sometimes encounter in complete sets of live financial statements. When learning the basic formulas in a textbook setting, it is much easier for you to learn the underlying concepts if complicating factors are assumed away. When dealing with live data, however, you must be able to incorporate the complexities or you risk arriving at an inappropriate conclusion. Part of the purpose of the **FRP** is to help you make that transition. When these slight modifications are introduced, the circumstances necessitating them are explained. The good news is that these modifications are usually very minor.

Another purpose of the **FRP** is to familiarize you with common sources of business and financial information. Employers expect that you are able to quickly and accurately obtain business and financial information about suppliers, customers, or competitors. Many of the assignments in this project will require you to use classic reference sources from the library or Internet that are used every day in the business world.

A third purpose of the **FRP** is to build teamwork skills. Many employers have made the remark, "You professors educate students one-at-a-time, but we employers work them in teams." Today, employers expect that you will have experience working closely on team-oriented projects. You may already know that teamwork skills take time and effort to develop. This is all part of your education, and failure to develop and extend your teamwork skills is just as dangerous to your career as failing to master personal computer and communication skills.

A fourth purpose of the **FRP** is to develop your writing skills, which is important for success in the business world. Depending on your professor's instructions, and based on your understanding and analysis of the material found in your annual report, you may prepare one of two written assignments:
(1) write one longer paper at the end of the **FRP**—Assignment 15; or
(2) write a series of up to four short memos (one to three pages, or a length set by your professor) as you complete Assignments 6, 9, 12 and 14.

Introduction to Memos

Memos are a primary and effective means of communication within an organization. Generally, they are brief and to the point as busy executives do not have time to wade through long and rambling reports. Typically, memos have a beginning similar to the one illustrated below, which appears in the upper left-hand corner. Further, headings are often used to allow the reader to quickly determine the major points.

Date memo is written.

To: Person(s) to whom the memo is addressed.
From: The person(s) writing the memo.
Subject: The purpose of the memo.

Note

Further discussion about writing memos can be found in May, Clair B. and Gordon S. May, *Effective Writing–A Handbook for Accountants*, Prentice-Hall, 1999, Ch. 9. Watch for the new Sixth Edition.

Based on different aspects of your **FRP** company, you will form opinions about the company which you may express in the form of a memo after Assignments 6, 9, 12 and 14. Each memo is described in a double-lined box on the last page of these assignments. To maintain a focus to your memos, the following scenario is provided, although your professor may develop another basis for the memos.

> You or your team are starting a firm to advise investors. A potential client has asked that you assist her in evaluating a company (your selected **FRP** company) which she might add to her investment portfolio. Also, based on the usefulness and quality of your memos and advice, she will determine whether or not to stay with your firm.

Each memo is another step in the development of your final memo after Assignment 14, which will culminate your research.

Preface to the Professor

The **FRP** has been used successfully in the sophomore-level introductory accounting course and in the MBA financial accounting course. As in the Second Edition, Internet web sites have been integrated into the assignments. Where appropriate, students are guided to the **Financial Reporting Project** (**FRP**) homepage at **baldwin.swcollege.com**. After selecting "assignments" the students can obtain relevant hot links to free web sites. All assignments, however, can still be completed using only traditional library resources.

This project is the result of many years of experimentation with students—that they successfully make the transition from classroom topics and textbook examples to the use and understanding of *real* financial statements. The **FRP** (which includes analysis of the SEC 10-K and the proxy statement) is designed to achieve this. An unanticipated side benefit of this project has been that students enjoy dealing with *live* financial information. It's often amazing how students will pore over the annual reports, proxy statements and SEC 10-Ks that they have received in the mail or downloaded from the Internet. When they run into complicated issues, their curiosity is piqued and they want to know more. Students are also intrigued by current readings. Each reading introduces an issue or issues related to the corresponding chapter of the text.

Student Teams. While this project is a valuable tool when completed by students working individually, its learning benefits are maximized when it is completed by student teams. The strategy is to assign a different company to each team in the class. Each student obtains his/her own copies of the annual report, 10-K and proxy statement. The assigned company can then be used for a variety of in-class and out-of-class team-based assignments. Each team member is expected to become an expert regarding his/her company and then contribute that knowledge to a written report prepared by the team. Teams can also make end-of-semester class presentations based on their written report. If you assign students to work individually, use Assignments 1-A and 4-A. If your students will work in teams, use Assignments 1-B and 4-B instead. All other assignments can be used by either individuals or teams. See the *Manual* for guidelines about teams.

Assignment Options. Unlike previous editions of the **FRP**, this one provides an alternative to the Capstone Project in Assignment 15—a series of up to four short memos as part of Assignments 6, 9, 12, and 14.

Other assignments ask the students to compare answers regarding their company with classmates. As an alternative, they may obtain the same information from other annual reports found on the Internet. Both options are discussed in more detail in the *Manual*.

Two lists of companies are included in the *Manual*. The first list utilizes the industry categories and more than 800 companies of the Fortune 500. The second incorporates additional companies of the Forbes 500 and NASDAQ 100, all in alphabetical order. Each company is identified by name, primary stock exchange, and ticker symbol.

The *Manual* also provides a variety of hints and suggestions regarding use of the **FRP**.

From the Authors. Thanks to many persons for their assistance in bringing this project to fruition. Students, for example, provided many helpful criticisms of early versions of many assignments. Faculty colleagues did the same. Special thanks to Sara Wilson of South-Western College Publishing who provided much encouragement and many helpful suggestions during critical stages of development. Special thanks also to Ethel Hock for formatting this Third Edition and preparing the camera-ready copy. All errors and omissions, however, are our personal responsibility.

We hope that you find this project helpful and useful. If you have suggestions for improvement, please call, write, or send e-mail. Your suggestions are welcome.

Bruce A. Baldwin
School of Management
Arizona State University West
P.O. Box 37100
Phoenix, Arizona   85069-7100

Phone: 602-543-6210
Fax: 602-543-6303
E-mail: bruce.baldwin@asu.edu

Clayton A. Hock
Department of Accountancy
Miami University
317-D Laws Hall
Oxford, OH   45056-1602

Phone: 513-529-6246
Fax: 513-529-4740
E-mail: hockca@muohio.edu

Table of Contents

Assignment 1-A
Choosing a Company
(for individual students)

The purpose of the **Financial Reporting Project** (**FRP**) is to apply the lessons of your accounting course to a real company. You will discover how the issues, topics, practices and procedures described in your textbook actually affect a company's financial statements.

The first step is to choose a company that you think you will find interesting and that you want to know more about. Choose carefully because you will work with this company on several assignments this term. Be sure to choose a publicly-held U.S. company so that its financial information will be readily available. (Publicly-held means that its stock is traded on a stock exchange.)

Because of the nature of their business and specialized accounting practices, it is usually best to avoid financial institutions, e.g., banks, as well as public utilities. Your professor may give you additional guidelines on choosing a company.

Identifying Companies from Which to Choose

Recognizing that your professor may have placed some limitations on your choice, here are some possible ways to go about identifying companies from which to choose.

1. You might first want to choose an industry that interests you. For example, a specific industry might be appealing because:

   a. Someone you know works in that industry or perhaps you have worked in a particular industry that you would like to learn more about.

   b. A company in that industry is located in your hometown or in a nearby location.

   c. You regularly purchase products from that industry (e.g., textbooks, clothing, or beverages).

   d. The industry might be one that could provide employment opportunities after graduation.

   e. The industry has been in the news lately, and you are interested in being better informed about the issues that were raised.

2. A good place to start is in your school's library. Following are five sources that provide information about many industries and specific information about individual firms in those industries.

   a. *Standard & Poor's Industry Surveys*, published by Standard & Poor's, Inc. This three-volume document is published every quarter and updated twice a year. It covers approximately 52 industries and more than 1,200 companies. In the front part of each volume you will find a section entitled the "Earnings Supplement." This section lists all of the industry categories and each of the companies within each industry.

b. *Value Line Investment Survey*, published by Value Line, Inc. This service is updated weekly and comes in three parts. The front page of Part 1, "Summary & Index," lists more than 90 industry categories along with the page number where information on each industry can be found. In Part 3 you will find the industry information as well as specific information about each company in each industry.

c. *Fortune* is a bi-weekly business magazine published by AOL Time Warner. Its annual listing of the 500 largest firms in the United States is referred to as the Fortune 500 and is probably the most widely cited listing of this type. The Fortune 500 usually is in the mid-April edition.

d. *Hoover's Handbook of American Business,* published by Hoover's, Inc., profiles 750 major U.S. companies, including overview, history, officers, location, products, and competitors.

e. *Standard Industrial Classification* (SIC) *Manual*, published by the U.S. Government Office of Management & Budget, organizes all businesses and industries in the United States into four-digit SIC codes. In the back of the volume is an alphabetical index of industry categories with the SIC code for each category. The front of the manual has a detailed description of each industry category. Use this manual to select an industry and its four-digit SIC code. After selecting an industry, go to the *Million Dollar Directory*, published by Dun & Bradstreet, Inc. The directory is a series of five volumes; look for the one labeled "Series Cross-Reference by Industry." This volume is organized by SIC code numbers. You will find many companies for whatever SIC code you have chosen along with each firm's mailing address and telephone number. (This information will be handy for Assignment 1-C.)

On the Internet

The Internet is a rich source of financial information. Throughout this book we provide references to many helpful sites. Convenient access is provided through the Baldwin homepage.

Go to **baldwin.swcollege.com**, select "assignments," and explore the hot links listed under Assignment 1-A.

Name _____   Professor _____

Course _____   Section _____

Completing Assignment 1-A – Choosing a Company

1. What is the name of the company you have chosen?

   _____

2. Which industry category does your firm represent?

   _____

3. Write several paragraphs describing how (and why) you chose the firm you did.
   Did you use any of the resources listed earlier in this assignment, or the
   Internet? Were they easy to use? Hard to use? Which one(s) would you
   recommend to friends if they had to complete this assignment? Discuss.

   Note: *Please think and plan carefully before writing. Readability, spelling,
   organization, grammar, and sentence structure will all be considered in grading
   your response.*

   _____
   _____
   _____
   _____
   _____
   _____
   _____
   _____
   _____
   _____
   _____
   _____
   _____
   _____
   _____
   _____
   _____

Assignment 1-B
Organizing Your Group
(for student teams)

The purpose of the **Financial Reporting Project** (**FRP**) is to apply the lessons of your accounting course to real companies. You will discover how the issues, topics, practices and procedures described in your textbook actually affect companies' financial reports.

Overview of the Group Project

Your professor has already assigned your group a company (or companies) on which to focus. The final output of this project will be an analysis of the company (or companies) assigned to you.

If your group is to evaluate several firms in the same industry, your first task will be to assign a specific company to each member of your group. This will be your first exercise in group decision making.

Each group member is expected to become very knowledgeable regarding one or all of your team's assigned companies. You will obtain the company's financial statements (see Assignment 1-C) and observe how your firm implements the principles and practices that you will learn in this course. Later in the course you will begin to analyze and evaluate your individual firm's financial stability and trends. Also you will conduct library research to further familiarize yourself with your company and the industry in which your firm competes. If team members have been assigned a different firm, the other members of your group will be doing the same thing for their firms (which compete with yours).

Each member will contribute his/her expertise regarding the assigned firm(s) to the group's report. Your group's project will be due on a date announced by your professor. There are more instructions on the group report and analysis in Assignment 15 if this is required.

You should review those instructions *very soon* and begin (as a team) to develop strategies for completion of the project.

Completing the Assignment

1. In the space provided on the next page, list the name, telephone number, and e-mail address (if any) of each member of your team. This listing will help you keep in contact during the course.

	Group Member Names	Phone Numbers	E-mail Addresses
a.	_____	_____	_____
b.	_____	_____	_____
c.	_____	_____	_____
d.	_____	_____	_____
e.	_____	_____	_____
f.	_____	_____	_____

2. Choose a name for your group and write it in the space provided. Feel free to be creative. For example, you might want to select a name that is a clever play-on-words regarding the name of your company or industry. Your professor will probably appreciate the humor.

    Group name _____

3. After completing this assignment (as a team) turn in one copy of the group information to your professor. Also, be sure that every team member has a complete set of the information in Number 1.

Name _____   Professor _____

Course _____   Section _____

Assignment 1-C
Obtaining Financial Statements

Most future assignments will be based on information contained in your company's Annual Report, its SEC Form 10-K, and its proxy statement. In this assignment you are to contact your assigned (or chosen) company to request the most recent copy of those items.

The Annual Report is a document that must be distributed to all shareholders every year. It contains the firm's financial statements as well as a variety of other required and optional information. Often it is a slick and glossy publication with color pictures of the executives, company facilities, and products. The SEC Form 10-K is the version of the annual report that must be filed annually with the Securities and Exchange Commission (SEC), an agency of the federal government in Washington, D.C. When you receive your firm's Annual Report and SEC 10-K you will notice that the two documents have many similarities but that they also have some striking differences.

The proxy statement is a document describing matters that will be discussed or voted on at the annual stockholders' meeting. It is also the device by which management of the corporation solicits your authorization (proxy) to vote your shares on its behalf. Of greatest interest, perhaps, is that proxy statements must provide detailed information about compensation of key executive personnel. (Ever wonder how much money the president of a large corporation is paid?)

Completing the Assignment

1. Contact your company by telephone, letter, or e-mail. You will need to go to your university library, community public library, or the Internet to obtain the mailing address, e-mail address, or telephone number. The address, and usually the phone number, can be obtained from the following sources:

   a. *Directory of Corporate Affiliations*, National Register Publishing Co.

   b. *Million Dollar Directory*, Dun & Bradstreet.

   c. *Q-File*, Q-Data Corporation.

   d. *Hoover's MasterList of Major U.S. Companies*, Hoover's, Inc.

   You may also be able to request a copy of your company's annual report at the company's web site, usually the company's name followed by ".com." Look under a heading such as *Investor Services* or *Investor Relations*.

> ## On the Internet
> Web sites at which you may be able to find out how to contact your company are listed on the Baldwin homepage.
>
> Go to **baldwin.swcollege.com**, select "assignments," and explore the hot links under Assignment 1-C.

2. The following hints will help you carry out this assignment.

   a. Companies usually have an Office of Investor Relations or Shareholder Relations. Write to, or telephone, that office. If your company has an Internet homepage, you may be able to send an e-mail request directly.

   b. Explain that you are a student at (identify your school) and that as part of an accounting class assignment this term you will be studying the firm and its financial information.

   c. Request a copy of the firm's most recent Annual Report, most recent SEC Form 10-K, and its most recent proxy statement. Be sure to tell them how much you appreciate their assistance. A little gratitude goes a long way in smoothing these requests. (Actually, most firms are very happy to provide these documents. They tend to think of you either as a potential investor, potential customer, or both.)

   d. Provide an *exact* mailing address. These documents are very important to you and you do not want to risk having them mishandled because of a vague address.

3. Record the following information regarding your request.

   a. Method of making the request (e.g., telephone, fax, letter, e-mail)

   _____

   b. Post office address or e-mail address of firm (if you sent a letter or e-mail)

   _____

   _____

   _____

   c. Phone number of firm (if you telephoned or faxed) _____

   d. Date of request for documents _____

Sample Letter

If you prefer to write a letter it could be similar to the following.

(Your Name and Address)

(Today's Date)

Investor Relations Department
Humble Pie Bakery Corporation
3652 Modesty Boulevard
Ovenhot, Arizona 00000

Director of Investor Relations:

I am a student at (name your school). As part of an accounting
class assignment this term I will be examining and analyzing the
financial reports of a major corporation.

I have chosen your firm and would like to study the financial
reports of your corporation as part of my class assignment. Would
you please assist me by sending me a copy of your most recent
Annual Report, most recent SEC 10-K, and most recent Proxy
Statement? Thank you very much for your help!

Sincerely,

(Signature)

(Your Name, typed)

Later Assignments

In later assignments you will compare information about your company with
information from the annual reports of your classmates or from annual reports
found on the Internet. The following instructions take you step-by-step to obtain
the financial information and proxy statement from the Internet that you could use
for comparison.

How to Download Financial Statements from the Internet
Using the Security and Exchange Commission's EDGAR database

1. Sign on the Internet and go to the following address:
   www.sec.gov/edaux/formlynx.htm
2. In the "Select the form" box, select **10-K**.
3. In the "Enter a company" box, type the name of the company you want, e.g.,
   General Motors.
4. In the "What data range?" box, select **Entire database**.
5. Click on the **Submit Choices** button.
6. When the next screen appears, you will probably see a list of documents.
   Select the latest 10-K report by placing the cursor on the company name next
   to the latest date and clicking on the name.
7. Wait for the document to load. Some documents are long and require several
   minutes.
8. Save the file to disk. **Do not print**. Some documents are over a hundred pages
   long.
9. Sign off the Internet.
10. Open the saved document in **Word** (or another word processor; all references
    here are to Word). The file is saved as a text file (.txt). In the File, Open menu,
    set the type of files to **All Files** to see the .txt files you have saved.
11. Select the entire document (in the Edit menu, click on **Select All**). Set the font
    to **Courier New** and the font size to **8**. In the File, Page Setup menu, set right
    and left margins to **.5 inches**. This adjustment usually will ensure each line
    will be readable. Do not reformat the document. If you do, you probably will
    not be able to read the financial statements without a lot of realigning of text.
12. Find the financial statements in the document. They usually appear near the
    end. You can use the Edit, Find menu to search for key words such as "finan-
    cial statements," "Income statement," "statement of earnings," etc. You must
    use trial and error, because companies use various terms for their statements.
13. Highlight the financial statements and accompanying notes that follow the
    statements, and print these pages (click on **Selection** under Page range in
    File, Print menu), or cut and paste them into a new document for later access.
14. Save the original 10-K document as a **Word** file for future reference.

Name _____   Professor _____

Course _____   Section _____

Assignment 2
Basic Company Information

Name of your company _____

The purpose of this assignment is to help you obtain background information about your firm. The first step toward understanding a firm's financial information is to understand the company itself.

Completing the Assignment

1. For each of the items below that you use in completing this assignment, be sure to indicate in the space provided the edition (or year of the edition) that you used. If some of the suggested references are not available in your library, your reference librarian may be able to suggest other sources that you could use instead.

Reference	**Edition Used**
a. *The Corporate Directory of U.S. Public Companies*, Walker's Western Research	_____
b. *Million Dollar Directory*, Dun & Bradstreet, Inc.	_____
c. *Mergent Corporate News Reports*, Mergent FIS (formerly *Moody's Industrial Manual*, Moody's Investors Service)	_____
d. *Standard & Poor's Register of Corporations, Directors, and Executives*, Standard & Poor's (S&P)	_____
e. *Standard & Poor's Corporation Records*, S&P	_____
f. *Directory of Corporate Affiliations*, National Register Publishing Company	_____
g. *America's Corporate Families*, Dun & Bradstreet, Inc.	_____

    > ### On the Internet
    > Sometimes different companies have similar names. To provide exact identification, web sites often request you to type in the company's stock ticker symbol, a one-to-five letter code under which the company's stock trades on the stock exchanges.

As soon as possible, identify your company's stock ticker symbol. It will make your search for information easier. Go to the Baldwin homepage at **baldwin.swcollege.com**, select "assignments," and explore the hot links listed under Assignment 2.

Note

Web sites appear or disappear suddenly. Sometimes data that *was* free suddenly requires a fee. We monitor the web and update the Baldwin homepage regularly to keep our list of free web sites as current as possible.

2. Use the library references listed on the prior page to obtain the information requested below and to answer the questions that follow.

   Note: *Please think and plan carefully before answering the questions. Readability, organization, spelling, grammar, and sentence structure will all be considered in grading your responses.*

   a. Basic company facts:

   1) Complete name of firm _____

   2) State in which company is incorporated _____

   3) Year in which the company was founded _____

   4) Primary and secondary SIC codes _____
      (For an explanation of SIC Codes, see page 15.)

   5) Independent auditor _____

   6) Stock exchange(s) where its shares are traded _____

      _____

   7) Stock ticker symbol _____

   b. Describe the products your company offers and type(s) of customers to whom those products are probably sold.

      _____

      _____

      _____

      _____

      _____

      _____

      _____

      _____

      _____

c. Is your company a large company? Identify several measures that could be used to describe the "size" of a company. How does your firm measure up on those attributes?

_____

_____

_____

_____

_____

_____

_____

_____

_____

d. Describe your company's Board of Directors as to age, gender, background, experience, etc.

_____

_____

_____

_____

_____

_____

_____

_____

e. Is your company part of a "group" of companies? For example, does it have subsidiaries? Is your firm a subsidiary of some other firm? Discuss.

_____

_____

_____

_____

_____

_____

_____

_____

_____

_____

3. What are the most interesting aspects of your company (or its industry) that
    you have discovered so far? Discuss.

_____

_____

_____

_____

_____

_____

_____

_____

_____

_____

_____

_____

_____

_____

_____

_____

_____

_____

_____

_____

_____

_____

_____

_____

Explanation of SIC Codes

The Standard Industrial Classification Code (SIC Code) is a simple coding system that is used to gather, classify and report information on U.S. businesses. It was devised by the U.S. government in the 1930s and has been updated periodically, most recently in 1987. The SIC system has been widely adopted as a standard for defining and analyzing industry structure. This system divides virtually all economic activity into 10 major categories:

Agriculture, Forestry and Fishing	01-09
Mining	10-14
Construction	15-17
Manufacturing	20-39
Transport, Communications, Utilities	40-49
Wholesale Trade	50-51
Retail Trade	52-59
Finance, Insurance, Real Estate	60-67
Services	70-89
Public Administration	90-97

The SIC system classifies each line of business into one of these ten categories and assigns a four digit code. The first two digits are referred to as the Major Group Code and describes the general nature of the activity. For example:

Major Group 78 . . . . Motion Pictures

The third and fourth digits of the SIC Code describe the specific activity.

7812	Motion Picture and Video Tape Production
7819	Services Allied to Motion Picture Production
7822	Motion Picture and Video Tape Distribution
7832	Motion Picture Theaters, Except Drive-In

Under the SIC system, many companies can be categorized under several "lines of business" and therefore are assigned several SIC Codes. The line of business which represents the largest percentage of sales is known as the Primary SIC; others are referred to as Secondary SICs.

Generally, when multiple SIC codes are listed for a single firm, they are presented in descending order of their percentage of the firm's sales volume. The primary SIC is listed first (largest percentage of sales) followed by secondary SICs in descending order of respective sales percentages.

The North American Industry Classification System (NAICS)

The SIC Codes are currently being replaced by the North American Industry Classification System (NAICS, pronounced "nakes") developed by the U.S., Canada and Mexico after the North American Free Trade Agreement (NAFTA). The NAICS reclassifies and regroups industries to better reflect the North American economy, now more service oriented and technological than manufacturing based, i.e., process rather than product.

The NAICS codes contain six digits rather than four. The first two, like the SIC

Codes, represent the general economic sector in which the industry is classified. The third designates the subsector; the fourth the industry group; and the fifth the NAICS industry. The sixth digit is unique in that it refers to the specific country's industry.

Though NAICS is said to be a better classification system, the conversion to its use has been slow. A major problem is that approximately half of the industries in the manufacturing sector of NAICS do not have comparable industries in the SIC system, impacting comparability of current and historic data. While the 1998 Annual Census of Manufactures used only the NAICS, the SEC's EDGAR database continues to use SIC Codes. Therefore you may be better off if you continue to use SIC Codes as well.

NAICS On the Internet

More information about the NAICS can be found on the NAICS Association website at **www.naics.com**.

To convert the older SIC Codes to the NAICS, go to the Arkansas Small Business Development Center website at **www.asbdc.ualr. edu/naics/**.

To see the 1998 Annual Survey of Manufactures, visit **www.census.gov/prod/2000pubs/m98-as1.pdf**.

Reading 2
Annuals Remain Top Info Source:
Investors Rate Annual over Financial Media or Analysts' Reports

Staff Reports

The vast majority of investors rate annual reports as the most important source on which to base an investment decision, according to a recent survey.

Some 91% of investors said that a company's annual report was the most credible source of information, above the financial media and analysts' reports, according to a survey by Research-Strategy-Management Inc. for the Public Relations Society of America.

Yet ironically, only 8% of Americans polled said they request such information first. Most tend to check a likely company's Web site, which was among the least credible sources in RSM's National Credibility Index.

"An annual report is fairly objective, straightforward and quite expert in terms of giving out company information," RSM President Ron Hinckley said.

The credibility of annual reports for investors suggests an increasing importance to the IR [Investor Relations] function, Hinckley said.

One of the most common problems companies have is clarifying revenue reports. The Securities and Exchange Commission is particularly stringent in this area, and many companies have been forced to go back and change their reporting.

"With the Internet making information available to more people, a recommendation would be for IROs [Investment Relations Officers] to reassess how they dealt with their annual report in terms of making it easier to understand," Hinckley said.

The credibility of annual reports is enhanced by objective reporting. The minute people get a sense of subjectivity in a corporate document, they tend to shy away from it.

"The findings suggest that the average American is far more attuned to the nuances of financial information than might have been presumed," PRSA President Jean Farinelli said. "Easy access to business news and information does not mean that the message is being swallowed whole."

In addition, the research indicated that a company's CFO was believed to be more credible than the company's CEO. Companies should bring the CFO on board to address the reader in the annual report and make sure that the information in the annual report is updated regularly on the Web site, PRSA Director of Brand Development Sally Mitchell advised.

Although investors seem to prefer annual reports, Hinckley noted that investors did not mention it automatically when asked for credible sources. Annual reports rated low as an immediately desirable source but high on credibility. "The inverse was the Internet which was highly recognized as a starting point for research but low on credibility," Hinckley said.

Supporting Brand Image

Much of an annual report's credibility is due to the SEC. Because companies have to file a 10-K with the Commission, investors are more likely to assume the contents of an annual report are reliable.

"Annual reports have a credible image. The perception is that there are legal aspects to writing annual reports so a company is not going to lie or provide misleading information," Mitchell said.

Although the Internet is not a trusted source, it is a good medium for broader research, according to Peter Wakeman, CEO of World Investor Link Inc., which sells companies and mutual funds access to a database of self-directed individual investors.

"It's primarily because the investor starts looking at a Web site or a financial newspaper as part of a broad search for information, perhaps about several companies," Wakeman said.

Before the Internet can be discounted entirely, it is important to note that there is a 15-point difference in its credibility ranking between investors who cited it as a credible source compared to those that didn't mention it until were asked about it. "People who use the Internet regularly are much more comfortable with its credibility as a source," Hinckley said.

IROs can woo investors by increasing the amount of information available on the company's Web site. "[Investors] want to get what they believe is factual information for investment purposes," Hinckley said. Annual reports, other financial information and the inclusion of specialist news sources were highly rated features on corporate Web sites.

Cosmetics are also important, and overall design of the Web site can effect investors' perception of a company. A user-friendly Web site can help enhance a company's image, Mitchell said.

"Companies should put their annual report on the Web site and make it very easy to find, quick to download and easy to understand," Mitchell said.

In addition, Mitchell suggests that IROs include news articles featuring the company on the Web site to provide more information to the investor.

Lack of Oversight

One of the reasons the Internet scored relatively low on credibility is likely to be due to the lack of checks and balances according to Mitchell.

"There's no editorial review board like print and broadcast journalism. There's no Good Housekeeping seal of approval for consumer protection. The public is responding to that," Mitchell said.

Despite overall poor credibility, it is unlikely that other news sources will surpass the Internet as the first place investors turn to for information.

"The Internet is available 24 hours a day, seven days a week. If someone is sitting around at 10:30 on a Sunday evening and they want information, they can log on and find it, whereas it's a much bigger effort to run down to the newsstand and try to select out of hundreds of magazines which one you want and then find an article that captures your interest," Mitchell said.

Internet chat rooms are the chief venue for investors who want to discuss their holdings, company news and other stock information. As expected, chat rooms were rated the poorest source of credible information due to a heavy amount of rumor and speculation, Mitchell said.

Television often rivals the Internet in terms of being a popular news medium, but only 3% rated TV news as a good information source, despite the popularity of financial news programs on CNBC and CNN. "People don't have that much faith in television. Thirty second sound bites are not things you put credibility into for assessment. It's not a prime source for people making investment decisions," Hinckley said.

Advertising also was rated toward the bottom. Internet, TV, and print advertisements all scored below 44 index points. "It's real easy as a PR professional to see this, mark it with a yellow highlighter and demand that the advertising budget be slashed and the PR budget be quadrupled," Mitchell said.

However, reading between the lines indicates a different picture. Advice from a family member had a rating of 68 index points which put it in the top 15.

"All opinions get formed over time and there are thousands of impressions that come at people from all different directions," Mitchell said.

But although the message of advertising is clearly getting through to some investors, it is not effective enough to justify the cost.

"A company can project the most well-targeted message possible, but if it is delivered by an ineffective source of information, then it hasn't gained anything," Mitchell said.

Investor Relations Business
April 3, 2000
pages 1, 14+

Question for Consideration

As a potential investor would you be more concerned about ease of access (Internet) or credibility (annual report)? Explain. What other sources of information would you most likely use? Why?

Exercise: *An Experiment in Business Reporting On the Internet* can be found on the FASB web site. Go to accounting.rutgers.edu/raw/fasb/tech/index.html and click on FauxCom Inc. Scroll down to the site map and navigate around the various parts of the reporting package. What is your overall assessment? What feature(s) do you particularly like or not like about the reporting package? Explain.

Assignment 3
The Economic, Social, Legal and Political Environment

This assignment sends you to the library (and/or to the Internet) to do some background reading about your firm. Financial statements are best understood when the reader comprehends fully the economic, social, legal and political environment in which the firm operates. The purpose of this assignment is for you to gain an understanding of that current environment. There may be important new legislation that has affected your firm, or perhaps there has been a recent management shakeup. New technology, new competitors, new social trends, or legal battles could all affect the general health of your firm.

Key References for this Assignment

Following is a sampling of bibliographic indexes that college and university libraries typically have available. Remember, this is just a sample. Not all libraries will have all of the these items and most libraries will have others. The following list is provided to help you get started. A major purpose of this assignment is to develop your skills in library (and/or Internet) research by gaining familiarity with typical sources of business information. Space has been provided for you to write in any additional sources you find and use.

Reference	Available in your library?	Did you use it?
a. *ABI-Inform*, UMI, Inc. (on CD-ROM)	_____	_____
b. *Accountants Index*, American Institute of Certified Public Accountants	_____	_____
c. *Business Newsbank*, Newsbank, Inc. (on CD-ROM)	_____	_____
d. *Business Periodicals Index*, H.W. Wilson Company	_____	_____
e. *Predicast F & S Index*, Predicasts	_____	_____
f. *The New York Times Index*, New York Times Co.	_____	_____
g. *The Wall Street Journal Index*, Dow Jones & Co.	_____	_____

Other References Used

h. _____

i. _____

On The Internet

Alternatively, or in addition to your library search, you may want to "surf the net" for background information about your firm.

Go to the Baldwin homepage at **baldwin.swcollege.com**, select "assignments," and explore the hot links listed under Assignment 3.

Completing the Assignment

1. Use the sources suggested above to identify recent articles about your firm. Generally you should focus on articles that are no more than two years old. Select two recent articles concerning your company (no more than one article from a single source listed above). Find the article, read it, and if you believe it conveys significant and interesting information, photocopy it (or download it) to turn in with this assignment.

    Note: *It is a serious breach of academic integrity to tear articles out of magazines that do not belong to you, e.g., those in the library. Please don't do it!*

2. Index (website) used to find article #1 _____

3. Citation for article #1

    a. Name of periodical _____

    b. Title of article _____

    c. Date of periodical _____

    d. Page numbers _____

4. Article analysis: Describe why this article is significant and interesting. Limit your response to no more than 100 words and use complete sentences.

    _____

    _____

    _____

    _____

    _____

    _____

    _____

_____

_____

_____

_____

_____

_____

_____

5. Index (website) used to find article #2 _____

6. Citation for article #2:

    a. Name of periodical _____

    b. Title of article _____

    c. Date of periodical _____

    d. Page numbers _____

7. Article analysis: Describe why this article is significant and interesting. Limit
    your response to no more than 100 words and use complete sentences.

    _____

    _____

    _____

    _____

    _____

    _____

    _____

    _____

    _____

    _____

    _____

    _____

    _____

8. Attach photocopies of the articles to this assignment.

Reading 3
The Politics of Accounting

By Grace Hinchman
FEI's vice president of government relations

No longer can the accounting profession rely on the Financial Accounting Standards Board and the Securities and Exchange Commission to modify U.S. accounting principles. Now, Capitol Hill wants to weigh in because, in large part, the high-technology industry has successfully used its newfound political clout to spur Congressional support for the New Economy business model.

Over the last couple of years, New Economy companies have increasingly been at odds with the detailed accounting requirements of today's financial reports. Some argue that New Economy businesses can't or won't adapt to traditional accounting standards, while others say that current financial statements are backwards—little more than holdovers from the Industrial Age. Generally, high-tech firms believe that traditional accounting rules do not properly recognize the true worth of high-technology intangible assets such as intellectual property, research and development costs, innovative processes and a highly skilled workforce.

A good example of the tensions between FASB and New Economy businesses is the FASB exposure draft on business combinations. FASB has tentatively proposed to eliminate pooling and require a 20-year amortization period for goodwill. Since high-tech companies have been unsuccessful so far in convincing FASB or the SEC to preserve pooling or allow for expensing of goodwill, they have taken their "constituent concerns" to Capitol Hill.

High-tech companies formed a coalition and retained several lobbyists to help develop a political strategy to defeat FASB's exposure draft. Beginning in the summer of 1999, they unleashed a coordinated effort on Capitol Hill. Activities included bus tours of Tysons Corner, Va., technology companies for Democratic Senators; letter-writing campaigns urging Congress to stop the FASB; Congressional hearings in which FASB Chairman Ed Jenkins was called to testify; Congressional staff trips to Silicon Valley to meet with high-tech executives; and strategically timed meetings with SEC Chairman Arthur Levitt and organizing fundraisers for members of key Congressional committees.

Pressure Hasn't Eased

It's no great surprise that these efforts have been successful. In July 1999, FASB decided to postpone indefinitely its consideration of the accounting treatment of purchased in-process research and development (IPR&D) costs—a key high-tech issue. Chairman Jenkins explained that FASB had concluded that "it was not possible to address purchased R&D costs separately from other R&D costs." Although IPR&D was not a part of the business combination project, Jenkins apparently thought he could get high-tech executives to blunt their Congressional campaign if he threw them a bone such as delaying IPR&D.

Unfortunately for FASB, the IPR&D bone wasn't enough. Congressional pressure has continued, including claims that the country's technological innovation and economic growth will stop dead in its tracks if the business combination exposure draft is implemented. In response, FASB has pushed back its planned implementation date from late 2000 to mid-2001 in hopes of cobbling together a compromise that will satisfy the high-tech forces while addressing some of FASB's technical accounting concerns.

Chairman Jenkins deserves all the credit for recognizing the need to engage with Congress and the high-tech community instead of ignoring them. Most of the FASB forces are ill-equipped to handle Capitol Hill's politicians and professional staff with the finesse and diplomacy required to satisfactorily resolve this political hot potato. Chairman Jenkins possesses those skills, and FASB is fortunate to have him.

The big unknown right now is what will Congress do, if anything, if a compromise isn't reached. Congress, to its credit, recognizes its own shortcomings in this area but feels duty-bound to provide as much assistance as possible to its constituents, and it wants to keep the country's economy booming. Congress could pass a strongly worded but nonbinding sense-of-the-Congress resolution. A more draconian result could be establishing Congressional oversight of FASB—the beginning of accounting standards regulation.

I anticipate that the former is possible sometime next year if FASB decides to eliminate pooling. However, the latter is far too distasteful and dangerous even for the most ardent high-tech supporters and New Economy promoters up on Capitol Hill to consider.

Financial Executive
November/December 2000
Page 65

Questions for Consideration

1. Who do you think can best set, monitor, and enforce accounting standards—the private sector (FASB) or the public sector (government)?

2. Do you think that the high-tech companies are justified in their efforts to influence accounting standards?

Assignment 4-A
Industry Information
(for individual students)

In prior assignments you have obtained a great deal of information about your chosen firm. By now you should have a good understanding of its background, its strengths, weaknesses, and current developments. This assignment shifts the focus from your specific firm to the industry of which your firm is a part. Overall trends within an industry generally have a large impact on the success of specific firms within the industry. As part of your prior reading you probably have obtained some insight into the nature of the industry in which your firm competes. This assignment is designed to further that understanding.

Key References for this Assignment

The following is a sampling of resources that college and university libraries typically have available. Remember, this is just a sample. Not all libraries will have all of these items and most libraries will have others. The following list is provided to help you get started. If you need assistance, ask the Reference Librarian. He/she will be glad to help. A major purpose of this assignment is to further develop your library (and/or Internet) research skills by gaining familiarity with additional classic sources of business information.

Category 1 Sources

The following are excellent sources of background information on industries.

1. *Standard & Poor's Industry Surveys*, published by Standard & Poor's, Inc. This three-volume document is published every quarter and updated twice a year. It covers approximately 52 industries and more than 1,200 companies.

2. *Value Line Investment Survey*, published by Value Line, Inc. This weekly service is comprised of three sections. The "Summary and Index" (Part 1) lists the page numbers in Part 3 where information regarding your industry category can be found. The *Value Line Investment Survey* provides detailed reports on approximately 1,700 companies across more than 90 industry groups.

3. *Predicast Forecasts*, published by Predicasts, Inc. This volume organizes its industry forecasts by SIC Code and provides estimates of industry sales and annual growth rates.

4. *Encyclopedia of American Industries*, published by Gale Research, provides detailed, comprehensive information on a wide range of industries in every realm of American business.

5. *U.S. Industry and Trade Outlook*, published by McGraw-Hill, contains information for more than 350 domestic industries and lists industry trends.

Category 2 Sources

These additional sources can be used to identify news articles that have an industry focus.

1. *ABI-Inform*, UMI, Inc. (on CD-ROM)

2. *Accountants Index*, American Institute of Certified Public Accountants

3. *Business Newsbank*, Newsbank, Inc. (on CD-ROM)

4. *Business Periodicals Index*, H.W. Wilson Company

5. *The New York Times Index*, New York Times Company

6. *The Wall Street Journal Index*, Dow-Jones & Company

7. Almost every industry has an industry periodical (such as *Progressive Grocer* in the supermarket business or *Advertising Age* in the advertising business). This would be a good source of information about issues facing the industry.

On the Internet

Alternatively, or in addition to your library search, you may want to "surf the net" for trends and developments affecting your company's industry.

Go to the Baldwin homepage at **baldwin.swcollege.com**, select "assignments," and explore the hot links listed under Assignment 4.

(The assignment continues on the next page.)

Name _____   Professor _____

Course _____   Section _____

Completing Assignment 4-A – Industry Information

Name of your company: _____

Industry category: _____

SIC Code for your company: _____   NAICS code: _____

1. Use one or more sources from Category 1 to familiarize yourself with trends and developments within your chosen industry.

   a. Which Category 1 source(s) did you consult? _____

   _____

   _____

   _____

   b. What major trends and developments are occurring in your industry? Summarize the information you obtained from Category 1 sources.

   _____

   _____

   _____

   _____

   _____

   _____

   _____

   _____

   _____

   _____

   _____

   _____

   _____

   _____

   _____

   _____

2. Use one or more of the Category 2 sources suggested on page 26 to identify recent articles about your industry. Generally you should focus on articles that are no more than two years old. Select two recent articles concerning your industry (no more than one article from a single index). Find the article, read it, and if you believe it conveys significant and interesting information, photocopy it to turn in with this assignment.

   a. Index used to find article #1 _____

   b. Citation for article #1

      1) Name of periodical _____

      2) Title of article _____

      3) Date of periodical _____

      4) Page numbers _____

   c. Article analysis: Describe why this article is significant and interesting. Limit your response to no more than 100 words and use complete sentences.

   _____

   _____

   _____

   _____

   _____

   _____

   _____

   _____

   _____

   _____

   _____

   _____

   d. Index used to find article #2 _____

   e. Citation for article #2:

      1) Name of periodical _____

      2) Title of article _____

      3) Date of periodical _____

      4) Page numbers _____

f.   Article analysis: Describe why this article is significant and interesting. Limit your response to no more than 100 words and use complete sentences.

_____

_____

_____

_____

_____

_____

_____

_____

_____

_____

_____

_____

_____

3. Attach photocopies of the articles to this assignment.

Note: _It is a serious breach of academic integrity to tear articles out of magazines that do not belong to you, e.g., those in the library. Please don't do it!_

Assignment 4-B
Industry Information
(for student teams)

In prior assignments you have obtained a great deal of information about your chosen firm. By now you should have a good understanding of its background, its strengths, weaknesses, and current developments. This assignment shifts the focus from your specific firm to the industry of which your firm is a part. Overall trends within an industry generally have a large impact on the success of specific firms within the industry. As part of your prior reading you probably have obtained some insight into the nature of the industry in which your firm competes. This assignment is designed to further that understanding.

Key References for this Assignment

The following is a sampling of resources that college and university libraries typically have available. Remember, this is just a sample. Not all libraries will have all of these items and most libraries will have others. The following list is provided to help you get started. If you need assistance, ask the Reference Librarian. He/she will be glad to help. A major purpose of this assignment is to further develop your library (and/or Internet) research skills by gaining familiarity with additional classic sources of business information.

Category 1 Sources

The following are excellent sources of background information on industries.

1. *Standard & Poor's Industry Surveys*, published by Standard & Poor's, Inc. This three-volume document is published every quarter and updated twice a year. It covers approximately 52 industries and more than 1,200 companies.

2. *Value Line Investment Survey*, published by Value Line, Inc. This weekly service is comprised of three sections. The "Summary and Index" (Part 1) lists the page numbers in Part 3 where information regarding your industry category can be found. The *Value Line Investment Survey* provides detailed reports on approximately 1,700 companies across more than 90 industry groups.

3. *Predicast Forecasts*, published by Predicasts, Inc. This volume organizes its industry forecasts by SIC Code and provides estimates of industry sales and annual growth rates.

4. *Encyclopedia of American Industries*, published by Gale Research, provides detailed, comprehensive information on a wide range of industries in every realm of American business.

5. *U.S. Industry and Trade Outlook*, published by McGraw-Hill, contains information for more than 350 domestic industries and lists industry trends.

Category 2 Sources

These additional sources can be used to identify news articles that have an industry focus.

1. *ABI-Inform*, UMI, Inc. (on CD-ROM)

2. *Accountants Index*, American Institute of Certified Public Accountants

3. *Business Newsbank*, Newsbank, Inc. (on CD-ROM)

4. *Business Periodicals Index*, H.W. Wilson Company

5. *The New York Times Index*, New York Times Company

6. *The Wall Street Journal Index*, Dow-Jones & Company

7. Almost every industry has an industry periodical (such as *Progressive Grocer* in the supermarket business or *Advertising Age* in the advertising business). This would be a good source of information about issues facing the industry.

On the Internet

Alternatively, or in addition to your library search, you may want to "surf the net" for trends and developments affecting your company's industry.

Go to the Baldwin homepage at **baldwin.swcollege.com**, select "assignments," and explore the hot links listed under Assignment 4.

(The assignment continues on the next page.)

Name _____   Professor _____

Course _____   Section _____

Completing Assignment 4-B – Industry Information

Name of your company: _____

Industry category: _____

SIC Code for your company: _____   NAICS code: _____

1. Use one or more sources from Category 1 to familiarize yourself with trends and developments within your chosen industry.

   a. Which Category 1 source(s) did you consult? _____

     _____

     _____

     _____

   b. What major trends and developments are occurring in your industry? Summarize the information you obtained from Category 1 sources.

     _____

     _____

     _____

     _____

     _____

     _____

     _____

     _____

     _____

     _____

     _____

     _____

     _____

2. Use one or more of the Category 2 sources suggested on page 32 to identify recent articles about your industry. Generally you should focus on articles that are no more than two years old. Select two recent articles concerning your industry (no more than one article from a single index). Find the article, read it, and if you believe it conveys significant and interesting information, photocopy it to turn in with this assignment.

   a. Index used to find article #1 _____

   b. Citation for article #1

       1) Name of periodical _____

       2) Title of article _____

       3) Date of periodical _____

       4) Page numbers _____

   c. Article analysis: Describe why this article is significant and interesting. Limit your response to no more than 100 words and use complete sentences.

   _____

   _____

   _____

   _____

   _____

   _____

   _____

   _____

   _____

   _____

   _____

   _____

   _____

   _____

   d. Index used to find article #2 _____

   e. Citation for article #2:

       1) Name of periodical _____

       2) Title of article _____

       3) Date of periodical _____

       4) Page numbers _____

f. Article analysis: Describe why this article is significant and interesting. Limit your response to no more than 100 words and use complete sentences.

_____

_____

_____

_____

_____

_____

_____

_____

_____

_____

_____

_____

3. Attach photocopies of the articles to this assignment.

Note: *It is a serious breach of academic integrity to tear articles out of magazines that do not belong to you, e.g., those in the library. Please don't do it!*

Reading 4
International rulemakers feel heat from U.S. officials

Reprinted with permission of *Accounting Today*.

By James R. Peterson

Pressure from the Securities and Exchange Commission could sound the death knell for the International Accounting Standards Committee, at least as it is presently constituted, if the international standards-setter doesn't clean up its act soon.

The SEC and the Financial Accounting Standards Board have long supported the work of the London-based IASC, which is supported by accounting organizations in nearly 100 countries. But now, the rapid globalization of markets is forcing both the SEC and FASB to pressure the IASC to either put up or shut up.

"The issue is whether we will have a level playing field for those companies who access our United States capital markets and whether U.S. executives will have the ability to participate in the development of international standards," FASB chairman Edmund Jenkins told executives at a conference of the Financial Executives Institute, in New York. "Right now, the SEC is evaluating whether the IASC standards are of sufficiently high quality to be used for U.S. reporting, and, in my view, they are not."

At the same time that SEC chief accountant Lynn Turner and Jenkins were speaking to financial executives in New York, an IASC strategy working party was meeting in Venice, Italy, to develop a restructuring plan in an effort to salvage the IASC's work. Both the SEC and FASB have endorsed the plan, for the time being.

But ultimately, final acceptance of a restructured IASC will depend on the selection of trustees and board members that the SEC and FASB each can live with.

"If the IASC cannot achieve high-quality standards, then we will look to see what type of new structure we will have to set up," Turner told the New York conference. That could take the form of either an international FASB or a morphing of the G4+1 study group into an international standards-setter.

The IASC had hoped to achieve a core set of international accounting standards by the Year 2000, but the goal has eluded it as the SEC, FASB and other groups have decried the common denominator quality of its standards-setting. Not only is there much more work to be done, there are other problems, as well.

Turner said it's not just about accounting standards, but the quality of the audits that are being done worldwide. He said that many foreign companies that are using IASC standards actually have not been complying with them in the way that they should be.

"So, even if we have high quality standards, unless someone is following them, it's just not going to do us any good," he said. "Also, many of the standards are new—going into effect in 1999 or thereafter—so we don't know whether the standards will work."

He said that international regulators are trying to develop an enforcement mechanism because they realize that companies aren't necessarily following the standards in their jurisdictions, and added that SEC officials have been meeting with the International Federation of Accountants in an effort to come up with some kind of mechanism that can be enforced on a world-wide basis.

"Rapid globalization has put us behind the eight ball," he said.

Globalization certainly has brought urgency to the work of standards setting. Today's "currency flows are tremendous," said Turner. "With the push of a button, cash is flowing across and in between countries extremely fast. There's something like $1.4 trillion in cash flows every day, which is something like four months' worth of the Gross National Product of the entire world."

Turner said, the SEC is also grappling with another important issue: Whether to accept the listings of foreign companies that use international accounting standards in the U.S. while maintaining U.S. registrants on the standards that FASB puts out.

FASB standards are thought to be impeccable by standards-setters worldwide, and several high-profile foreign corporations already employ them.

"We at FASB believe that, ultimately, we should have one global standards-setter and one global financial reporting system," said Jenkins. "It's the only efficient way of doing things as U.S. companies seek acquisitions outside the U.S. and U.S. companies seek to involve global investors in their companies."

Jenkins summed up by saying, "But global standards must have the same high quality as we enjoy in the United States, and they must be developed in the same independent and open due process as U.S. standards."

Accounting Today
December 13, 1999 – January 2, 2000
Pages 5 and 75

Questions for Consideration

1. Do you think that the SEC and FASB have legitimate reasons for ***not*** endorsing the IASC's current standards? Explain.

2. Why is the enforcement of IASC standards so important?

Assignment 5
Initial Review of Annual Report and Financial Statements

Name of your company: _____

By now you should have received the Annual Report (plus SEC 10-K and proxy statement) you requested from your company. The purpose of this assignment is to review and understand the basic information that is reported in your company's Annual Report with primary emphasis on the financial statements.

Organization of the Annual Report

In general, you will find Annual Reports organized into the six different sections discussed below.

1. **Financial Highlights** – Somewhere in the first few pages or so you will find a summary of financial highlights covering as many as 10 or 20 years. Often this section contains a variety of charts and graphs. These data are not financial statements but merely a shorthand summary of the firm over a number of years.

2. **The Company and Its Products** – Near the beginning of the report, there is usually a fairly lengthy section about the company and its products. (If the company has had a good year, there will probably be lots of color pictures of the executives. If the company had a bad year, they might leave out pictures of the executives altogether.) This section of the report includes mostly public relations-type information. It's a chance for the company to brag about its products, people, and activities.

3. **Management Discussion and Analysis** – Following the public relations section of the Annual Report, you will find a section titled "Management's Discussion and Analysis." Often this section is referred to in the business press by its initials, the MD&A. Here, management is required to identify significant events, trends and developments affecting the firm and to discuss management's thinking on these matters.

4. **Financial Statements and the Notes to the Financial Statements** – Following the MD&A, you should find the financial statements and the accompanying notes. Generally, there will be a balance sheet, income statement, statement of cash flows, and a statement of stockholders' equity. Often, each financial statement will have the word "Consolidated" in its title to indicate that the corporation

owns one or more subsidiaries and that the financial results of the subsidiaries have been combined with those of the parent company to produce a single set of financial statements. The Notes are an integral part of the financial statements because they disclose the accounting methods used by the firm, provide additional detail regarding certain amounts on the face of the financial statements, and disclose additional matters not otherwise revealed by the financial statements. Financial statements without the accompanying notes comprise incomplete disclosure and can be misleading.

5. **Statement of Management Responsibility and the Report of the Independent Accountants (or Auditor's Report)** – Read them carefully. These statements reveal (1) who is responsible for the content of the financial statements and (2) whether the financial statements present fairly the financial situation of the firm.

6. **Basic Company Facts** – Following the Notes to the Financial Statements there are usually two or three pages of basic facts about the company, e.g., list of officers and directors, stock exchange listing, state of incorporation.

Completing the Assignment

1. Read the Management Discussion and Analysis (MD&A) section. What is the general tone of management's comments in this section? Was the most recent year a positive or negative experience for the company? Does management appear optimistic or pessimistic about the future? Discuss.

_____

_____

_____

_____

_____

_____

_____

_____

_____

_____

_____

_____

_____

_____

_____

2. The Income Statement

  a. What format was used to prepare your firm's income statement? (Check one)

  _____ Single-step

  _____ Multiple-step

  Hint: *If gross margin (also called gross profit) is reported on the income statement, it's the multiple-step format. Otherwise, the single-step format has been used.*

  b. Determine whether any of the following "special items" appear on the most recent income statement. They would appear near the end. Indicate below whether the item appears and (if it appears) indicate whether it increased or decreased net income. Then explain the underlying event or transaction that caused the item to arise.

	Item present?	Increase	Decrease
1) Discontinued operations	_____	_____	_____

_____

_____

_____

2) Extraordinary gain (or loss)	_____	_____	_____

_____

_____

_____

3) Cumulative effect of a change in accounting principle	_____	_____	_____

_____

_____

_____

  c. Using your judgment, list the *major* items of revenue and expense that are reported on your company's most recent income statement. For each item, indicate whether it is a revenue or an expense. Do not include any of the special items from Part b above.

	Revenue	Expense
1) _____	_____	_____
2) _____	_____	_____
3) _____	_____	_____
4) _____	_____	_____
5) _____	_____	_____

3. The Balance Sheet

    a. Which of the following terms describes the balance sheet as reported by your firm? (Check those that apply.)

        _____ Classified balance sheet (i.e., assets are segregated into categories)

        _____ Comparative balance sheet (i.e., more than one year of data is presented)

    b. All publicly held companies are required to prepare a three-year comparative income statement and a two-year balance sheet. Why do you think that comparative financial statements are required?

        _____

        _____

    c. If your company presented a classified balance sheet, identify the amounts your firm reported for each of the following categories and the percentage of total assets that each represents.

	Amount	Percent
1) Current assets	_____	_____
2) Property, plant, and equipment	_____	_____
3) Other long-term assets	_____	_____
4) Current liabilities	_____	_____
5) Long-term liabilities	_____	_____
6) Contributed capital	_____	_____
7) Retained earnings	_____	_____

Note

If you were a creditor of a firm (i.e., the firm owed you money) you would be interested in whether the firm had enough resources to pay you when your bill came due. Two indicators of a firm's ability to pay its bills as they become due are (1) the amount of working capital (sometimes called net working capital), and (2) the current ratio (sometimes called the working capital ratio).

Working capital (WC) is the cushion by which total current assets exceed total current liabilities.

$$\text{WC} = \text{current assets - current liabilities}$$

The current ratio (CR) reveals how many dollars of current assets are available to pay off each dollar of current liabilities.

$$\text{CR} = \frac{\text{current assets}}{\text{current liabilities}}$$

---

d. What amount of working capital did your company have as of the date of its two most recent balance sheets?

   Important: *If your firm didn't prepare a classified balance sheet, you can't compute the amount of working capital or the current ratio. If that's the case, skip to No. 4.*

	Most Recent Balance Sheet	**Next Most Recent Balance Sheet**
Working capital	_____	_____

e. What was the current ratio, also known as the working capital ratio, at the end of the two most recent years? For comparison to other firms, check with five classmates (who are analyzing different firms) to see what their results were. Record those results below along with those of your firm. List the names of each comparative firm.

   Alternative

   As an alternative to comparing your company to those of your classmates, you may want to use four or five other companies' financial statements that you get from the Internet. These companies can be used in Assignments 6, 8, 9, 11 and 14 and can be from either your industry or different industries.

   Check with your professor to make sure this alternative is acceptable.

	Most Recent Year	**Next Most Recent Year**
Your firm _____	_____	_____
_____	_____	_____
_____	_____	_____
_____	_____	_____
_____	_____	_____
_____	_____	_____

f. How does your firm appear to compare to the other firms you listed above regarding its ability to pay current liabilities as they become due?

   _____

   _____

   _____

   _____

   _____

   _____

   _____

   _____

4. The Statement of Cash Flows

    a. Which format does your company use to report the statement of cash flows? (check one)

        _____ Direct format   (The operating activities section begins with a Direct format line such as "Cash received from customers.")

        _____ Indirect format (The operating activities section begins with a line such as "Net income" or "Net loss" and then proceeds to add and subtract items from that amount.)

    b. In the spaces following, fill-in the proper summary amounts from your company's most recent statement of cash flows. If any of the four categories represented a net cash outflow, show that amount in parentheses.

        1) Net cash inflow (outflow) from *operating* activities   _____

        2) Net cash inflow (outflow) from *financing* activities   _____

            List the two largest transactions

            a) _____

            b) _____

        3) Net cash inflow (outflow) from *investing* activities   _____

            List the two largest transactions

            a) _____

            b) _____

        4) Net increase (decrease) in cash, or sometimes labeled net change in cash and cash equivalents, for the year   _____

    c. Now go back to the balance sheet and fill-in the following amounts that are reported for Cash (under the assets category).

        1) Current year's ending cash balance   _____

        2) Prior year's ending cash balance   _____

        3) Change in cash balance during the current year   _____

    d. Does the number on line c.3) above match the number on line b.4) above? (check one)

        1) _____ Yes   _____ No

        Hint: *They should match. This is an example of financial statement* articulation, *which means that numbers reported on one financial statement are related to numbers on the other statements.*

        2) If the amounts do not match, by how much do they differ?

            _____

5. The Statement of Stockholders' Equity

    a. Did your company include a statement of stockholders' equity with the rest of its financial statements? (check one)

        _____ Yes

        _____ No   (If no, ignore part b.)

    b. Carefully review the most recent year's data on the statement of stockholders' equity. Were there any significant changes in the amounts comprising stockholders' equity between the beginning of the year and the end of the year? If so, complete the table below for the significant changes. In the right-most column, use parentheses to indicate a balance that decreased.

    Ignore changes that you judge to be insignificant. If your company had no significant changes in the amounts comprising stockholders' equity, note that on the first line.

Statement of Stockholders' Equity Accounts	Balance at Beginning of Year	Balance at End of Year	Change in Balance During Year
_____	_____	_____	_____
_____	_____	_____	_____
_____	_____	_____	_____
_____	_____	_____	_____
_____	_____	_____	_____
_____	_____	_____	_____

6. Notes to the Financial Statements

    a. The first footnote is usually labeled something like "Summary of Significant Accounting Policies." It explains which accounting alternative that management selected to handle a particular type of transaction. Give two examples of an accounting policy disclosed in this note.

        1) _____

        2) _____

    b. What type of information is revealed in the remaining footnotes?

    _____

    _____

    _____

    _____

    _____

7. Statement of Management Responsibility and the Report of Independent Accountants

   Differentiate between the roles of a company's management and its auditor with respect to the financial statements.

   _____

   _____

   _____

   _____

   _____

   _____

   _____

8. Articulation of Financial Statements

   Articulation of Financial Statements refers to information on one financial statement being related to information on another financial statement. Find an additional example of articulation in your company's financial statements beyond the example involving cash from No. 4.d. Describe it.

   _____

   _____

   _____

   _____

   _____

   _____

   _____

   _____

   _____

Reading 5
Accounting Fraud: Learning from the Wrongs

By Paul Sweeney
Freelance business writer based in New York

Sunbeam Corp. will long be remembered as more than a household name for electric appliances and camping equipment. It will also be notable for more than a decade of mismanagement and dubious experiments in ruthless cost-cutting and wholesale firings.

For years to come, the name "Sunbeam" will bring to mind a company that relied on questionable accounting gimmicks and outright fraud in sacrificing the company's reputation on the altar of enhanced earnings and a jacked-up stock price.

It happened under the direction of disgraced CEO Albert Dunlap—the notorious, take-no-prison West Point graduate and veteran corporate downsizer unaffectionately known as "Chainsaw Al"—who put company managers under orders to get the stock price up at any cost. One way to do that, as it turned out, was to report robust sales of electric blankets in the summer and barbecue grills in late autumn.

Eventually, earnings woes and Dunlap's bluster prompted his ouster by an aroused board of directors in June 1998. That was followed shortly by the replacement of accounting firm Arthur Andersen and a series of Investigations and shareholders lawsuits, most of which are still pending.

Sunbeam joins an ignominious cluster of companies—Rite Aid, CUC International (now part of Cendant Corp.), Livent, Oxford Health Plans, Phar-Mor, Miniscribe and, most recently, MicroStrategies—in business's hall of shame. All of these companies have one depressing feature in common: top managers who, whether out of desperation or greed, apparently turned to accounting trickery to manufacture imaginary sales and other revenues and pump up earnings, sometimes over a period of years. Writing in *The Wall Street Journal,* one pundit recently reckoned that just three recent fraud cases—Sunbeam, CUC and Oxford—burned shareholders for an aggregate $34 billion when the troubles surfaced and the stocks plummeted.

Chief financial officers and comptrollers at such companies may be under duress and persistent pressure to look the other way—though published studies suggest that, regrettably, they are often involved. Outside directors likely have no clue about any shenanigans. But there are plenty of instances where someone aware of the fraud stepped forward. "Most frauds are not found by fraud investigations," says Dan Jackson, president of Jackson and Rhodes, a Dallas-based accounting firm. "It's usually because of a disgruntled employee, a dissatisfied vendor or someone with a conscience."

These days, just the suggestion that a company may have accounting irregularities is enough to drive down its stock price, notes Robert Willens, an accounting analyst at Lehman Brothers. He cites the case of Tyco International, a well-managed company that makes home-security and alarms systems but which was rumored to have accounting problems by the *Tice Report*, a markets newsletter published by short-seller David Tice. After Tice raised suspicions, the company lost one-third of its value, although the Securities and Exchange Commission later gave it a clean bill of health.

"It doesn't seem to matter whether it's the SEC or some newsletter, everyone seems willing to sell a stock now even if there's just a hint of questionable practices," Willens says. "Nobody wants to own the next Cendant or Sunbeam."

Accounting irregularities are getting the attention of Corporate America for another important reason: allegations that companies are not conforming to Generally Accepted Accounting Principles have become a growth industry for lawyers. A study issued in August by PricewaterhouseCoopers calls the role that accounting allegations now play in federal securities litigation "striking."

It wasn't supposed to happen this way. Congress passed the Private Securities Litigation Reform Act of 1995 to give companies relief from what were seen as a rash of frivolous lawsuits. The law provided corporations with breathing room in the form of "safe-harbor" provisions that allowed businesses to make "forward-looking" statements without fear of being sued if earnings predictions or growth projections failed to materialize.

Yet the number of class-action lawsuits on behalf of shareholders has returned to pre-reform act levels— and the No. 1 reason, the PWC study concludes, is assertions of accounting improprieties. Figures compiled by the Big Five accounting firm show that in 1999, 108 of the 205 private class-action lawsuits— more than 50 percent—involved allegations of accounting irregularities.

That figure represents the highest percentage of accounting-related charges made during any single year of the decade. It is also nearly double the share that accounting-related charges played during 1995— the year before the safe-harbor legislation took effect—when just 25 percent of the 185 cases were accounting-related.

The new law clearly did not provide a safe harbor for material misstatements arising in companies' audited financial statements, notes Harvey Kelly, a partner at PWC's financial advisory services group in New York who provided commentary for the just-released study. "The act provided some protection to the companies if things turned out

differently, as long as they warned people about forward-looking statements," Kelly says. "But if the results don't meet the accounting rules, you can make more of a case." Under the law, he adds, "you're allowed to sue."

PricewaterhouseCoopers figures show that in 1999, more than 50 percent of private class-action lawsuits involved allegations of accounting irregularities.

The study reports that many of the GAAP violation cases have been brought under the antifraud provisions—Rule 10b-5— of the Securities Act of 1934. The study also found that in 1999, more than 50 percent of accounting-related claims involved charges that companies mishandled revenue recognition. In 40 percent of the GAAP-related claims, the study adds, companies overstated their assets. In addition, it found that irregularities in purchase accounting, liabilities and accounting estimates were also prevalent among the allegations.

Sunbeam is a good example of a company that engaged in creative revenue recognition. A review of the company's books by auditors from Deloitte & Touche and Arthur Andersen in the autumn of 1998—it took nearly four months for them to unravel what "Chainsaw Al" biographer John A. Byrne called the "dirty bag" of accounting complications—found that the company's recorded profits of $109.4 million in 1997 were illusory. Restated, the earnings amounted to a mere $38.7 million.

How did Dunlap and his buccaneering allies at Sunbeam do it? One strategy was Sunbeam's practice of "bill-and-hold," in which retailers like Wal-Mart and Costco, in exchange for a discount, agreed to purchase shipments of grills six months before they were needed and pay for them six months later—not within 30 days, as the SEC's guidelines for bill-and-hold accounting state. The grills were also parked over the winter months in warehouses leased by Sunbeam because suppliers had no room for them. A similar program had been put in place during the summer of 1997 for electric blankets.

Bill-and-hold is "a device that auditors need to be very careful of," says Paul Regan, a forensic accountant at Hemming Morse in San Francisco, whose resume includes work on such fraud cases as MiniScribe and Phar-Mor. "Overstating revenues and concealing obsolete inventory happen in a majority of misstated financial statements," he adds. "You see it particularly in instances where there is major financial statement manipulation involving products or services, including software."

At CUC International—a shopping club company that merged with hotel and car rental company HFS to form Cendant— phony accounting entries created the illusion of millions in profits, making CUC a darling of Wall Street analysts for more than a decade. When the mess was uncovered in the wake of the merger, it cost investors—including corporate pensions, mutual funds and 401(k) plans—$19 billion. The fraud is also landing three top financial executives in prison, including CUC's former chief financial officer, 40-year-old Cosmo Corigliano, who faces up to 10 years in jail. The SEC is bringing additional charges against the trio, as well as several other former executives.

What is so astonishing, observers have noted, is that such a massive fraud continued for so long. Corigliano was a 23-year-old, newly minted accountant fresh from Ernst & Whinney when he went to work for CUC in 1983, the year the company went public. The fraud was not discovered until after the merger in 1997. "The activities had started about then [1983]," Corigliano told a judge in June, when he pleaded guilty to fraud charges. Accountants Ernst & Young have settled a $300 million lawsuit with Cendant, which alleged that the firm should have spotted the fraud at CUC.

The New York law firm Willkie Farr & Gallagher and Arthur Andersen combined to investigate the accounting irregularities at Cendant and reported their findings to the audit committee of the company's board of directors. The report says earnings of former CUC businesses were overstated by approximately $500 million before taxes during the 1995–1997 period alone. Investigators noted the use of such questionable devices as irregular revenue recognition, understatement of reserves, delays in recording credits and recording of fictitious receivables.

The use of a restructuring reserve fund amounting to several hundred million dollars was an especially notable feature. Rather than covering one-time costs

associated with takeovers, the reserve fund became a vehicle for concealing ordinary business expenses and losses and a pot that could be dipped into to meet expected earnings results. "For companies into 'cookbooks' and 'sins books,'" Regan says—citing the jargon frequently used at companies employing accounting scams—"this is a relatively common vehicle."

Rite Aid presents another case where efforts to unravel accounting irregularities have proven to be a Herculean task. In July, Rite Aid restated its books and admitted that it had overstated profits during the prior two years by more than $1 billion. After spending more than $50 million in accounting fees to pore over its murky financial records, according to *The Wall Street Journal*, the company also reported a net loss of $1.14 billion for the fiscal year ending in February.

A commission investigating instances of fraudulent financial reporting found that audit committees and boards of the companies it analyzed appeared to be weak.

Both the SEC and the U.S. Attorney's Office are looking into whether the irregularities at Rite Aid officially constitute fraud. Meanwhile, the company's former top management—including its ex-CEO, former president and former CFO—as well as its accounting firm, KPMG, are all being sued in a class-action brought on behalf of shareholders. The stock, which sold as high as $24 in mid-1999, was

under $5 in early August.

Accounting experts say that Rite Aid engaged in just about every form of accounting impropriety available. For example, it capitalized ordinary expenses to inflate current income and hid depreciation expenses by counting them as construction-in-progress, according to the *Journal*. The biggest adjustments—more than $500 million over two years—came in the category of inventory and cost of goods sold. Among other things, Rite Aid boosted income by recording credits from vendors that hadn't been earned.

Rite Aid differs from Cendant and Sunbeam in one important respect: Its accounting firm, KPMG, questioned the integrity of the company's books and resigned from the account. At Sunbeam, the improprieties were discovered only after Dunlap got fired by a restive board. At Cendant, they came to light when an employee who had been participating in the subterfuge finally blew the whistle.

While accounting fraud remains the exception—even at 108 cases in 1999, the number of shareholders lawsuits involving accounting is still "quite a small portion of companies that file financial statements," says PWC's Kelly—certain patterns frequently crop up. One is the presence of a tough and powerful CEO who frightens subordinates, notes San Francisco-based accountant Regan. "It's a fairly common theme to have a personality like 'Chainsaw Al'—a domineering bully whom people are fearful of. They are afraid of coming up short of the established goals."

This observation is borne out by a report from the Committee of Sponsoring Organizations of the Treadway Commission, issued in March 1999. The panel studied 200 companies charged with fraudulent financial reporting from 1987–1997. Among its findings was the observation that top executives were frequently involved. In 83 percent of the cases, the report found, either the CEO or the chief financial officer—or both—were associated with financial statement fraud.

Common Characteristics

The report, "Fraudulent Financial Reporting: 1987–1997," also noted that the audit committees and boards of the companies it analyzed appeared to be weak. Most audit committees seldom met, and boards of directors were dominated by insiders and others with close connections to the company. The report concluded, too, that "a significant portion of the companies were owned by the founders and board members."

Several observers have noted that both patterns were particularly apparent at Cendant, where "you did not have independent directors, and both companies [CUC and HFS] were entrepreneurial and controlled by their founders," notes John Coffee, a securities expert at Columbia University Law School. Adds corporate gadfly and shareholder activist Nell Minow, a Washington, D.C-based attorney: "What struck me about Cendant was that, over the same period of time, its compensation committee met eight times but its audit committee met only twice."

As most investigations show, the motive for the fraud was to drive up a company's stock price and satisfy Wall Street's expectations. For that reason, many observers fret that corporate controls are more necessary than ever, now that the bull market can no longer be relied on to lift stocks in general. In the meantime, the get-rich-quick mentality at many Internet and New Economy start-ups, coupled with prevailing compensation schemes that involve stock and stock option grants, create an ideal breeding ground for aggressive financial reporting. This is especially true in an era when the auditing function is seen as a commodity, and accounting firms rely on the integrity of management.

Says law professor Coffee: "Often you're dealing with companies founded by 20-year-olds who are impatient with the Old Economy's ways of doing things. They don't understand that accounting manipulation affects your credibility for a long, long time. You don't recover once you've been found to have fabricated your numbers."

Tips for Avoiding Fraud

- Develop strong audit committees and outside directors.
- Beware of a preoccupation with reporting strong earnings, which can be a slippery slope.
- Institute a series of checks and balances: Different people should make a sale, book a sale and collect the money.
- Steer clear of gimmicks like reserve funds, capitalizing ordinary expenses and excessive "bill-and-hold" periods.
- Be careful with revenue recognition and purchase accounting.
- Have 800 numbers or other lines of communication available for potential whistleblowers.

Financial Executive
September/October 2000
Pages 18 – 20 and 22

Questions for Consideration

1. List at least four techniques that companies have used to falsify their accounting reports. Why might management feel that they need to engage in such manipulative practices?

2. Explain the potential effects of accounting gimmickry on both stockholders and management.

Name _____   Professor _____

Course _____   Section _____

Assignment 6
The SEC 10-K Report and Proxy Statement

The Securities and Exchange Commission (SEC), an agency of the federal government, was established by the Securities Exchange Act of 1934 to promote full-disclosure of all material financial facts and other information concerning securities offered for public sale. The SEC's primary mission is to protect investors and maintain the integrity of the securities markets. Nothing can prevent the purchase of risky or low-quality securities, but the SEC strives to make sure that investors are fully informed as to the nature of their investment.

The purpose of this assignment is for you to understand the similarities and differences between a company's Annual Report to Shareholders and its SEC Form 10-K which must be submitted to the SEC annually. In addition, you will review your firm's proxy statement and evaluate certain information from it.

Name of your company: _____

In general, companies having assets of $10 million or more and 500 or more stockholders are subject to SEC regulation if their securities (e.g., stocks or bonds) are traded publicly. Principal among those regulations is the filing of regular public reports with the Commission. While there are more than a dozen different reporting forms used by SEC registrants, the three most commonly used reporting documents are the following SEC forms.

- 10-Q – the quarterly report to the SEC

- 8-K – an as-needed report of unscheduled events or corporate changes important to shareholders or the SEC. For example, when a company changes independent auditors it must announce that event by filing an 8-K with the SEC.

- 10-K – the annual report to the SEC

The 10-K is, by far, the best known of the SEC-required reports. In essence, it is a special version of the company's Annual Report. In this assignment you will learn how these are similar and how these are different. You will also discover that interesting information is disclosed in the proxy statement.

(The assignment continues on the next page.)

> ## On the Internet
>
> Since 1996 the SEC has required all public companies to make their required SEC filings (e.g., 10-Qs, 8-Ks, 10-Ks) electronically. These filings are then posted to the SEC's web site within 24 hours. This system is called EDGAR, which stands for Electronic Data Gathering, Analysis, and Retrieval.
>
> You can access EDGAR by going to the Baldwin homepage at **baldwin.swcollege.com**, selecting "assignments," and looking under Assignment 6; or follow the directions on page 10.

Completing the Assignment

The outline of this assignment is as follows. First, you are to identify each of the required sections of the SEC 10-K and indicate where they appear in your company's 10-K report. Second, you are asked to assess the similarities and differences between the information contained in your company's SEC 10-K and its Annual Report. Third, you are asked to record certain specific information about your company that is disclosed on the proxy statement.

1. The SEC 10-K Report is comprised of 14 items organized into four parts as shown below. Review your company's SEC Form 10-K and note the page(s) where each item is reported.

	Page(s) Where Item Is Reported
Part I	
Item 1. Business	_____
Item 2. Properties	_____
Item 3. Legal Proceedings	_____
Item 4. Submission of Matters to Vote of Security Holders	_____
Part II	
Item 5. Market for the Registrant's Common Equity and Related Stockholder Matters	_____
Item 6. Selected Financial Data	_____
Item 7. Management's Discussion and Analysis of Financial Condition and Results of Operations	_____
Item 8. Financial Statements and Supplementary Data	_____
Item 9. Changes in and Disagreements with Accountants on Accounting and Financial Disclosure	_____

Part III

Item 10. Directors and Executive Officers of the Registrant _____

Item 11. Executive Compensation _____

Item 12. Security Ownership of Certain Beneficial
Owners and Management _____

Item 13. Certain Relationships and Related Transactions _____

Part IV

Item 14. Exhibits, Financial Statement Schedules,
and Reports on Form 8-K _____

2. After carefully comparing your firm's annual report to its SEC 10-K, answer the
following questions.

a. What information did you find in both the annual report and the SEC 10-K?

_____

_____

_____

_____

_____

_____

_____

_____

b. What information is found in one document that is not found in the other?

_____

_____

_____

_____

_____

_____

_____

_____

c. Why do you think these differences exist?

_____

_____

_____

_____

_____

_____

_____

_____

_____

3. Answer the following questions based on information disclosed in the proxy statement.

   a. Identify the date and location of the stockholders' meeting announced in the proxy statement.

   Date _____

   Location _____

   b. Briefly describe the proposals, issues, or topics that were scheduled for action at the stockholders' meeting.

   _____

   _____

   _____

   _____

   _____

   c. For your firm's highest paid executive, compute the total dollar amount of compensation (e.g., salary + bonus + etc.) that he/she received from the company in each of the last three years.

   For perspective about how your firm's highest paid executive compares to those of other firms, check with five classmates (who are studying different firms than you) and record their information below also. To conserve space, record information in thousands of dollars (000's).

   Alternative

   As an alternative to comparing your company's highest paid executive to those of your classmates' companies, you may want to compare with the companies you used in No. 3.e. of Assignment 5.

   Check with your professor to make sure this option is acceptable.

Highest Paid Executive's Total Compensation	**Your Firm**	**C O M P A R A T I V E F I R M S**				
		Firm 1	**Firm 2**	**Firm 3**	**Firm 4**	**Firm 5**
Most recent year	_____	_____	_____	_____	_____	_____
Next most recent year	_____	_____	_____	_____	_____	_____
Next most recent year	_____	_____	_____	_____	_____	_____

d. How does the total compensation of your firm's highest-paid executive compare to the highest-paid executives of your comparative firms over the past three years? Discuss.

_____

_____

_____

_____

_____

_____

_____

_____

_____

e. Inspect the stock performance graph near the end of the proxy statement. How does the price performance of the company's stock compare to that of other companies? Does the trend in stock returns match the trend in compensation being earned by the company's top executives? Discuss.

_____

_____

_____

_____

_____

_____

_____

_____

_____

_____

_____

4. Optional Memo No. 1 – Company Background

Having completed the first six assignments of the **FRP**, you have acquired sufficient information about your company and its industry to prepare the first memo to your client. Though there are four separate memos, together they will develop an overall assessment of your company.

For format see page -iv- in the Preface or follow your professor's instructions.

Guide for Memo No. 1

a. State your *initial reaction* about your company , i.e., favorable or unfavorable.

   In your analysis you may want to consider the following:

   ▸ your company's industry;

   ▸ its major products or services;

   ▸ general economic and political environment; and

   ▸ your company's position in the industry, i.e., does it appear to be a leader (pro-active) or follower (reactionary)?

b. Does your company's overall disclosure system—its annual report and SEC filings (10-K and proxy)—appear to contain sufficient information to allow you to gain a working knowledge about your company?

   Explain.

Reading 6
The SEC Wants To Open the Info Vault

Reprinted with permission of *AOL Time Warner*.

By Lee Clifford

Less-than-golden rule — Regulation FD sounds great on paper, but will it help investors know more about the companies they own?

Now that the SEC's new Regulation FD has gone into effect and every Wall Street analyst, journalist, lawyer, and policy wonk has a different take on what it will actually mean, you're probably knee-deep in opinions and confused about the bottom line on how it will affect you. FD (which stands for "Fair Disclosure" and went into effect Oct. 23) mandates that any news with the potential to move a stock must be released to everyone at the same time. Trouble is, every constituency has a different viewpoint. To clear all the hot air and what-if scenarios, here's a FORTUNE reality check on what the various parties are saying—and what you can really believe.

The SEC: For years, the SEC argues, analysts and big institutions had a heady advantage over regular investors. If a company expected soft earnings, for example, management could give those lucky insiders a heads-up, potentially allowing them to, as the rule states, "make a profit or avoid a loss at the expense of those kept in the dark." Now the playing field will—at least ostensibly—be level.

Reality Check: "Arthur Levitt said, 'Give me a rule,' and he got a rule," says Lou Thompson, president of the National Investor Relations Institute (NIRI). "But there are some unintended consequences." The biggest brouhaha is over whether Regulation FD's vague language will actually do away with selective disclosure or simply lead to company paranoia and an information drought. "It's hard to say whether there will be less disclosure overall," says Elizabeth Mackay, chief investment strategist at Bear Stearns. "But certainly it will be less continuous." Expect a lot of tight-lipped execs, especially around earnings season.

Analysts: "We're going to have to rely less on companies and do more legwork on our own," says Mark Marcon, an equity analyst at First Union Securities. "Companies are currently unsure about how to act in this environment, so they're taking the safest course possible and revealing significantly less than ever before." Previously companies would review analyst estimates and provide "guidance" to keep their numbers from getting too far afield (in addition to the pavement pounding that good analysts were already doing). That gave them a fuller picture in writing their research reports. But with a black hole on corporate information, says one analyst, "you can get blind-sided every quarter."

Reality Check: In many respects the analysts are right. According to Thompson at NIRI, 75% of the companies in his organization used to hold one-on-one freewheeling meetings with analysts. Now, he says, "that kind of guidance is history." Expect to see analysts spending more time schmoozing with suppliers and distributors or talking to retail employees. Plan on earnings estimates all over the board for the fourth quarter and a shakeout that separates analysts who do their homework from those who don't.

Public Companies: Our lawyers have "instilled the fear of God in us," noted Richard Galanti, CFO of Costco, during the company's third-quarter-earnings conference call. The major goal for companies during the first few months of Regulation FD will be to make sure they don't become a prosecution test case. Says Mackay: "No one wants to be the poster child." Until there is one, caution reigns.

Reality Check: It's all about delivering earnings. If companies are reluctant to talk numbers between regularly scheduled meetings and conference calls, there's an even greater premium on reliable management teams— that is, those that can give accurate early estimates, then make their numbers and earn the trust of the Street. Companies will be wary of guiding earnings publicly to analysts, the media, and individuals throughout the quarter—they could face shareholder lawsuits if that guidance turns out to be wrong.

The Little Guys: During the SEC's comment period before the rule took effect, it received about 6,000 letters and e-mails, mostly from individual investors, in support of the rule. "Many felt that selective disclosure was indistinguishable from insider trading in its effect on the market and investors, and expressed surprise that existing law did not already prohibit this practice," reads the text of the regulation. The notion that it will put retail investors on a par with a high-level analyst at Goldman Sachs or a fund manager at Fidelity is an appealing one.

Reality Check: There's already a payoff for individuals: Quarterly earnings calls that used to be open only to bigwigs are increasingly open to investors in listen-only mode or simulcast on the Internet, and companies are already loading their Web sites with more information as well.

Still, there could be a very real downside—more earnings surprises and greater stock volatility. And therein lies the rub: It's great to be on a par with Goldman and Fidelity, but not if you're all getting blindsided together.

Fortune
November 13, 2000
Page 434

Questions for Consideration

1. Is it necessarily bad if analysts are privileged to financial information?

2. What subsequent problems might be caused by Regulation FD?

Exercise: Many companies now carry conference calls over the Internet. To learn more about them, use one of the following sites to listen to a conference call, either live or archived.

- BestCalls at www.bestcalls.com

- Yahoo Broadcast at www.broadcast.com. Under Categories select Business & Finance, then Earnings Calls.

Note: *Some services require registration, but many do not. If you prefer not to register, choose another company's conference call.*

Assignment 7
The Accounting Profession

The purpose of this assignment is to learn about the independent accounting firm that audited your company's financial statements. You will also have an opportunity to further develop your library research skills. (Make no mistake about it, these skills are valued by employers. They expect you to know how to find business information about potential customers, suppliers, competitors, or firms that might be potential acquisitions.)

Key References for this Assignment

Category 1 Sources

1. *Directory of Leading Private Companies*, National Register Publishing Company

2. *Million Dollar Directory*, Dun & Bradstreet (volumes labeled "America's Leading Public & Private Companies")

Category 2 Sources

1. *ABI-Inform*, UMI, Inc. (on CD-ROM)

2. *Accountants Index*, American Institute of Certified Public Accountants

3. *Business Newsbank*, Newsbank, Inc. (on CD-ROM)

4. *Business Periodicals Index*, H.W. Wilson Company

5. *Predicast F&S Index*, Predicasts

6. *The New York Times Index*, New York Times Company

7. *The Wall Street Journal Index*, Dow-Jones & Company

Completing the Assignment

1. Name of your company _____

2. Name of your company's auditor _____

3. Size of the accounting firm

   The purpose of this section is to demonstrate that the public accounting firms that audit large U.S. companies are, generally, very large companies themselves. The "Big Five" accounting firms (Andersen; Deloitte and Touche; Ernst and Young; KPMG Peat Marwick; and PricewaterhouseCoopers) all had revenues in 1999 of between $3.3 and $6.9 billion dollars. Odds are that your firm was audited by one of these companies.

   Use either of the Key References in Category 1 to determine the following information about your firm's independent auditor. If your library does not have either of these references, the Reference Librarian probably can suggest alternative sources from which to obtain the data.

   ## On the Internet
   The information needed for this assignment is usually included at the accounting firm's website, although you may have to hunt for it.

   You can access your auditor's website by going to the Baldwin homepage at **baldwin.swcollege.com.** Select "assignments" and then Assignment 7.

   ---

   a. Where is the home office of your company's auditor?

   _____

   b. How many employees does the accounting firm have? _____

   c. Indicate whether this is the number of U.S. employees, employees worldwide, or whether this cannot be determined.

   _____

   The year for which this information pertains _____

   d. What is the annual revenue of the accounting firm that audited your corporation?

   _____

   The year for which this information pertains _____

   e. What services does your accounting firm offer besides auditing (now referred to as "assurance")?

   _____

   _____

   _____

   _____

   _____

4. Current issues facing your company's independent auditor

   Use one or more of the Key References in Category 2 (or the Internet) to identify recent articles about your company's independent auditor. Generally, focus on articles that are no more than two years old. Select two recent articles concerning your firm's auditor (no more than one article from a single index). Find articles that you believe convey significant and interesting information. Photocopy them to turn in with this assignment.

   a. Index used to find article #1 _____

   b. Citation for article #1

      1) Name of periodical _____

      2) Date of article _____

      3) Title of article _____

      4) Page numbers _____

   c. Article analysis

      Why is this article significant and interesting? Use complete sentences and limit your response to no more than 100 words.

      _____

      _____

      _____

      _____

      _____

      _____

      _____

      _____

      _____

      _____

      _____

      _____

      _____

      _____

      _____

      _____

      _____

      _____

    d. Index used to find article #2 _____

    e. Citation for article #2

        1) Name of periodical _____

        2) Date of article _____

        3) Title of article _____

        4) Page numbers _____

    f. Article analysis

      Why is this article significant and interesting? Use complete sentences and limit your response to no more than 100 words.

_____

_____

_____

_____

_____

_____

_____

_____

_____

_____

_____

_____

_____

_____

_____

_____

_____

5. Attach photocopies of the articles to this assignment.

    Note: *It is a serious breach of academic integrity to tear articles out of magazines that do not belong to you, e.g., those in the library. Please don't do it!*

Reading 7
'Going Concerns': Did Accountants Fail To Flag Problems at Dot-Com Casualties?

By Jonathan Weil
The Wall Street Journal Staff Reporter

Theo Francis, contributor

It's a going concern. But where is it going—out of business?

Look closely at nearly any company's annual financial statements, and you'll notice an obscure yet important qualifier. They are prepared on the presumption that the company is a "going concern"—that is, that it will continue as a business for at least another 12 months. And if an auditor has substantial doubt about a client's ability to continue as a going concern, it must say so in its report on the company's financial statements.

Investors often take those warnings, commonly called "going-concern clauses," to mean "run for the hills," and the inclusion of one can kill a company's plans to go public. Next month, as most companies file annual reports, dozens of flailing dot-coms are expected to disclose they have been tagged with that dreaded boilerplate.

But what about last year's crop of failed dot-coms? Of the 10 publicly owned dot-coms whose financial problems forced them to cease operations or file bankruptcy-court proceedings, only three had going-concern clauses at the time they shut down. And one of those three didn't have a going-concern clause in its annual report last spring, but instead got one from its auditor three months later—after the stock had tanked. Among the flame-outs that sported clean auditor opinions: **Pets.com**, **Quepasa.com** and **MotherNature.com**. All 10 were audited by Big Five accounting firms. (In addition to these 10 publicly traded companies, dozens of others that are still operating were delisted from stock exchanges, and many closely held dot-coms also filed for bankruptcy.)

In retrospect, critics say, there were early signs that the businesses weren't sustainable, including their reliance on external financing, rather than money generated by their own operations, to stay afloat. "You wonder where some of the skepticism was," says Mike Willenborg, an accounting professor at the University of Connecticut. "It makes you think that the auditors just felt these companies could keep raising money if they needed to."

For their part, the auditing firms say confidentiality rules preclude them from discussing details of specific audits. They note that nearly all 10 audits occurred in early 2000, before the technology-stock bubble popped in March. And auditors say they couldn't have anticipated the collapse that left so many capital-starved start-ups to die.

Consider the state of Pets.com, the company with the sock-puppet mascot, just before it went public in February 2000 with a clean **Ernst & Young** audit opinion from the month before. By the end of 1999, about 10 months after its inception, the company had spent 55.3 million, mostly on TV ads, to sell goods that cost $13.4 million for $5.8 million. The company's prospectus did predict that Pets.com, which was intentionally losing money to gain market share, would have at least 12 months' worth of cash after its IPO.

But it also warned it would "need to raise additional funds, and these funds may not be available to us when we need them. If we cannot raise additional funds when we need them, our business could fail." Further, the company said it expected to rack up losses for at least four years. The company on Nov. 4 announced it was closing its operations.

"The audit of the company was completed in accordance with all appropriate regulatory guidelines and represented the auditors' best judgment at the time," says Larry Parnell, an Ernst & Young spokesman. "In general, 10 months in the life of an Internet company in the year 2000 was a lifetime. The dot-com capital markets in the spring had a tremendous impact on a lot of companies, and that couldn't have been foreseen by anyone." Former Pets.com officials either decline to comment or couldn't be reached.

Indeed, under the auditing standards published by the American Institute of Certified Public Accountants and written by the auditing profession, the fact that a company goes under within a year of receiving a clean auditor opinion "does not, in itself, indicate inadequate performance" by an auditor. Further, the absence of a going-concern clause "should not be viewed as providing assurance as to an entity's ability to continue as a going concern," a point that over the years appears to have been lost on many investors.

The standards place responsibility on auditors to identify trends—recurring operating losses or negative operating cash flow, for instance—that may raise substantial doubt about a company's ability to survive until its next fiscal year. And when doubts surface, auditors are supposed to consider management's plans to mitigate the doubts. For money-losing dot-coms, the key considerations typically have been whether they could cut enough expenses or raise enough capital to stay in business.

But rather than questioning the sustainability of the bubble at a time when some dot-coms had stock-market valuations of several hundred times their revenues, critics say many auditors appear to have presumed the capital markets would remain

buoyant. "For anybody to have assumed a continuation of those aberrant, irrational conditions was in itself irrational and unjustifiable, whether it was an auditor, a board member or an investor," says Gary Lutin, a former investment banker who runs forums on financial-reporting practices for the New York Society of Security Analysts. In fact, the current auditing standards provide no guidance about how firm a company's financing commitments must be to pass muster.

In all 10 companies' filings, the management-discussion sections contained strong cautions. But those came from the companies and their lawyers—not the auditors, who are responsible only for evaluating the financial statements. Auditors' harsh words can carry a lot more oomph, because investors often see the sky-is-falling language contained in many companies' risk disclosures merely as lawsuit protection.

Ernst & Young, the Pets.com auditor, did issue a going-concern opinion for **Garden.com**, which shut down in November. However, because the company had a June 30 fiscal year, the opinion letter wasn't publicly filed until October.

PricewaterhouseCoopers had issued a going-concern opinion for **Value America** early last year in the company's annual report. The online retailer filed for Chapter 11 bankruptcy protection in August. But another client, **Streamline.com**, ceased operations in November without a going-concern clause.

Pricewaterhouse partner Jay Brodish declines to discuss either

company, but says that going-concern judgments are "a subjective exercise." He says that many dot-coms that closed last year might have had enough cash to survive 12 months but decided instead to wind down operations and distribute remaining cash to shareholders; he doesn't feel auditors should be criticized in such cases.

Arthur Andersen had three dot-com clients that went under last year: **ZipLink**, MotherNature.com and **ReSourcePhoenix.com**. All three had clean audit opinions when they filed their annual reports in early 2000, but the accounting firm tagged ReSourcePhoenix.com in June, reissuing its opinion with a going-concern clause when the online financial-services company filed a registration statement to raise more money.

In its annual report for 1999, MotherNature.com said it believed it had enough cash to last through the end of 2000, but added that additional financing likely would be needed before year's end or sooner, and that such financing was uncertain. The company's former chief executive, Michael Barach, says Andersen officials never discussed the possibility of a going-concern clause with him, but that they might have with the company's chief financial officer at the time, Michael Bayer, who declines to comment.

Dick Deiter, an Andersen partner in Boston and a member of the U.S. Auditing Standards Board, also emphasizes that going-concern decisions are a judgment call, declining to discuss the Andersen clients. "Our ability to predict, in terms of what is going to happen in the future, is no greater than the capital markets," he says. "I think auditors looked at these things awfully carefully. I don't necessarily agree that the judgments were wrong."

KPMG officials decline to comment. The firm gave clean audit opinions in early 2000 for Quepasa.com and **Mortgage. com**, both of which closed in the fourth quarter, and **Caredata.-com**, which filed for Chapter 7 bankruptcy in November. Hired in January 2000, KPMG was Quepasa.com's fourth auditor in 12 months, and the previous auditors didn't issue going concern opinions, either. When Quepasa. com filed a new registration statement in September so that some insiders could sell stock, KPMG allowed the company to cite its clean audit opinion from early 2000. Former Quepasa. com executives didn't return phone calls.

Going Concern, Going... Gone

"Going concern" clauses, in which auditors raise substantial doubt about a company's ability to stay in business for at least 12 months, were rare among dot-com companies that shut down or filed for bankruptcy last year. Here are dot-coms that folded in 2000 without going-concern clauses in their most recent auditor reports.

COMPANY	AUDITOR	STATUS
Caredata.com	KPMG	Filed Chapter 7 bankruptcy in November
Mortgage.com	KPMG	Announced closing in October
MotherNature.com	Arthur Andersen	Announced liquidation in October
Pets.com	Ernst & Young	Announced closing in November
Quepasa.com	KPMG	Announced liquidation in December
Streamline.com	PricewaterhouseCoopers	Ceased operations in November
Ziplink	Arthur Andersen	Announced closing in November

Sources: WSJ research, SEC filings

The Wall Street Journal
February 9, 2001
Pages C1 – C2

Questions for Consideration

1. Do you think that determining a company as a "going-concern" is as subjective as the auditors claim? What should auditors look for when evaluating a dot-com company?

2. The article describes auditors as lax because they did not include a "going-concern clause" in their report. Do you think that the auditors were justified in their claim that they followed professional auditing practices and regulations? Explain.

Assignment 8
The Income Statement

Name of your company _____

The purpose of this assignment is to obtain an in-depth understanding of your company's income statement as shown in the annual report and SEC 10-K. Information will be reviewed regarding revenues, expenses, income taxes, "special items," and subsequent events. In addition, you will conduct a basic financial analysis of the income statement.

Completing the assignment

1. Summarize the basic information on your company's income statements for the most recent three years. If an item was not reported, indicate by placing NA (for not applicable) in the space provided.

Basic Income Statement Information	Most Recent Year	Next Most Recent Year	Second Most Recent Year
a. Sales (total revenues)	_____	_____	_____
b. Cost of goods sold (CGS)	_____	_____	_____
c. Gross margin, profit or income	_____	_____	_____
d. Total other revenues, expenses, gains and losses (other than CGS)	_____	_____	_____
e. Income (loss) before taxes	_____	_____	_____
f. Income taxes	_____	_____	_____
g. Net income (loss)	_____	_____	_____
h. Comprehensive income	_____	_____	_____

This might be reported on a separate schedule rather than on the face of the income statement.

2. "Special items" are not typical and do not appear on all income statements. Identify any special items that appear on your company's income statements:

   ▸ income (or loss) from discontinued operations,

   ▸ extraordinary gain (or loss), and

   ▸ cumulative effect of a change in accounting principle.

67

If any of these special items appeared on any of the income statements for the last three years, check the item, indicate the year and the amount, and explain the underlying event/transaction that caused the item to arise.

Hint: *These events usually are explained in the Notes to the Financial Statements.*

a. _____ Income (or loss) from discontinued operations

　　　Year _____　　Amount _____

_____

_____

_____

_____

_____

_____

_____

_____

b. _____ Extraordinary gain (or loss)

　　　Year _____　　Amount _____

_____

_____

_____

_____

_____

_____

_____

_____

c. _____ Cumulative effect of a change in accounting principle

　　　Year _____　　Amount _____

_____

_____

_____

_____

_____

_____

_____

_____

> **Note**
>
> Earnings per share (EPS) is one of the most commonly used measures of a company's profitability. In its simplest form, EPS is calculated by dividing net income by the number of common shares outstanding. Though an intuitive concept, the computation can become quite complex.
>
> Two EPS figures—*basic* and *diluted*—are required to be disclosed on the income statement. They differ essentially in the number of shares considered outstanding.
>
> ▸ Basic EPS uses only those shares actually outstanding during the period.
>
> ▸ Diluted EPS uses shares outstanding as well as shares that could become outstanding under certain circumstances, e.g., stock options are exercised.

3. Find your company's Net Income EPS for the current year.

    a. Indicate each EPS and the number of shares used to calculate them.

        1) Basic EPS   _____ ;   Number of shares _____

        2) Diluted EPS _____ ;   Number of shares _____

    b. If your basic and diluted EPS figures differ, by how much do they differ?

        _____ What reason(s) can you give for this difference?

        Hint*: Reasons for the difference are normally found in the EPS footnote.*

        _____

        _____

        _____

        _____

        _____

        _____

4. In the Notes to the Financial Statements there should be a section with a title such as "Income Taxes." Read that carefully before completing the following section.

    a. What is the federal tax rate on corporations? _____
        (often called the *statutory tax rate*)

    b. What *effective tax rate* (sometimes called the *actual tax rate*) did your firm pay? _____

c. If the firm's *effective* or *actual tax rate* was different from the *federal* or *statutory rate,* list up to three items that caused them to differ.

_____

_____

_____

d. What was the firm's total income tax expense (in dollars) for the most recent year? _____

Note

Deferred taxes can be tax liabilities or tax assets.

▸ *Deferred tax liabilities* will be paid on profits which the company has reported on its income statement but that don't need to be paid to the government until some future date.

▸ *Deferred tax assets* represent taxes that have been paid ahead of time.

---

e. Check which type(s) of deferred taxes your company had.

_____ Deferred tax assets

_____ Deferred tax liabilities

f. Did your company have short-term and/or long-term deferred tax assets/ liabilities?

_____ Short-term

_____ Long-term

If your company had both, which is more significant? _____

g. Did the amount of your company's most significant deferred tax asset/ liability increase or decrease during the most recent year?

_____

h. By what amount did deferred taxes change from the prior year?

_____

i. List up to three examples of temporary differences that caused your firm to report deferred taxes.

_____

_____

_____

> **Note**
>
> A *subsequent event* is a significant event or transaction that occurs after the balance sheet date but before the annual report is distributed, e.g., the obtaining of a large contract or an unfavorable result from a major lawsuit. Failure to disclose this type of event could render the financial statements misleading.

5. Did your firm disclose any subsequent events? If so, briefly describe them.

   Hint: *They usually are reported in one of the last notes to the financial statements.*

   _____

   _____

   _____

   _____

   _____

   _____

   _____

   _____

   _____

   _____

> **Note**
>
> To determine a company's profitability trends, a percentage analysis of successive years' income statements is often prepared. This analysis frequently is referred to as preparation of *common-size income statements*. In addition, profit margins usually are computed and compared to the profit margin data of other firms.
>
> On a common-size income statement, each item is expressed as a percentage of net sales revenue. Sales revenue is arbitrarily set to equal 100% and everything else is related to it. For example, if cost of goods sold were $300 and sales were $400, cost of goods sold would be listed on the common-size income statement as 75% ($300/$400).
>
> Every item on the income statement is divided by sales. This type of statement will reveal specific trends in revenue and expense items across the years that otherwise would be obscured by growing (or decreasing) sales.

6. Prepare a percentage analysis (common-size income statements) for the most recent three years. Special items, such as discontinued operations, extraordinary items, and cumulative effects are not included in the analysis because they are not expected to recur.

   a. Complete the table below

Income Statement Item	Most Recent Year (% of Sales)	Next Most Recent Year (% of Sales)	Second Most Recent Year (% of Sales)
Sales revenue	100%	100%	100%
Cost of goods sold	_____	_____	_____
Gross margin	_____	_____	_____
Operating expenses	_____	_____	_____
_____	_____	_____	_____
_____	_____	_____	_____
_____	_____	_____	_____
_____	_____	_____	_____
Total operating expenses	_____	_____	_____
Operating income	_____	_____	_____
Other (non-operating) revenues, expenses, gains and losses			
_____	_____	_____	_____
_____	_____	_____	_____
_____	_____	_____	_____
Income before taxes	_____	_____	_____
Provision for income taxes	_____	_____	_____
Income before special items (i.e., before discontinued operations, extraordinary items, or cumulative effect)	_____	_____	_____

   b. From the information in the table above, identify the significant data points or trends that you observe over the three years.

   _____

   _____

   _____

   _____

   _____

_____
_____
_____
_____
_____
_____
_____
_____
_____
_____
_____
_____
_____

7. Summarize your firm's profit margins that you computed in No. 6.a. for each of the last three years.

	Most Recent Year	Next Most Recent Year	Second Most Recent Year
Gross profit margin % (gross margin/sales revenue)	_____	_____	_____
Operating profit margin % (operating income/sales revenue)	_____	_____	_____
Net profit margin % (net income/sales revenue)	_____	_____	_____

8. For perspective, compare your company's profit margins for the most recent year to those computed by classmates for their firms' most recent year.

Alternative

As an alternative to comparing your company's profit margins to those of your classmates, you may want to compare with the companies that you used in No. 3.e. of Assignment 5.

Check with your professor to make sure this alternative is acceptable.

	Your Firm	COMPARATIVE FIRMS Firm 1	Firm 2	Firm 3	Firm 4	Firm 5
Gross profit margin %	_____	_____	_____	_____	_____	_____
Operating profit margin %	_____	_____	_____	_____	_____	_____
Net profit margin %	_____	_____	_____	_____	_____	_____

9. How do your firm's margins correlate to those of your comparative firms? Are they high, low, or about the same? Is there anything specific about your firm, its industry, or your comparative companies or industries that would tend to explain the differences between your company's margins and those of the other firms? Discuss. Also, how would you describe the trend in your company's margins over the past three years?

    _____

    _____

    _____

    _____

    _____

    _____

    _____

    _____

    _____

    _____

    _____

    _____

    _____

    _____

    _____

    _____

10. Other common measures of profitability are the *return on assets* and *return on equity*. They are measures of efficiency that compare net income to the amount of assets and equity used to generate that income. The higher the returns, the more efficient was the use of assets and equity.

    a. Compute your firm's return on assets and return on equity for the most recent year using the following formulas.

        Note: *The exact formulas used to compute these ratios vary slightly among financial analysts.*

        $$\text{Return on assets} = \frac{\text{net income}}{\text{average total assets}^*}$$

        $$\text{Return on assets} = \underline{\hspace{4cm}}$$

$$\text{Return on equity} = \frac{\text{net income}}{\text{average stockholders' equity} *}$$

$$\text{Return on equity} = \underline{\hspace{5cm}}$$

$$* \quad \frac{\text{beginning balance} + \text{ending balance}}{2}$$

b. Compare your company's returns to those of your comparative firms.

	Your Firm	COMPARATIVE FIRMS				
		Firm 1	Firm 2	Firm 3	Firm 4	Firm 5
Return on assets	_____	_____	_____	_____	_____	_____
Return on equity	_____	_____	_____	_____	_____	_____

c. Assume this year's returns are representative of normal results. Do you think your company is an attractive investment? Discuss.

_____

_____

_____

_____

_____

_____

_____

_____

_____

On the Internet

To compare your company's profits (computed in No. 7) and profitability (computed in No. 10) with your company's industry, visit the Baldwin homepage at **baldwin.swcollege.com**, click on "assignments" and follow the instructions for Assignment 8.

Reading 8
What the Earnings Reports Don't Tell You

By Susan Scherreik

Here's how to find the real story behind the numbers.

The curtain is rising on the third-quarter-earnings drama, and the setting is ominous: slower economic growth, higher oil prices, and a weak and stumbling euro. U.S. corporations will be hard-pressed to deliver crowd-pleasing profits in this scenario, and so now more than ever companies are likely to resort to various accounting games—all perfectly legal—to puff up their profits and win over the audience.

Over the past few years, investment managers and accounting professionals have complained increasingly about the ploys that companies sometimes use to boost their profits: making selective disclosures in earnings releases, paying expenses with stock options, or bolstering the bottom line by taking investment profits when operating profits fall short. "We'll see companies playing the same games as before, only more so," predicts Fred Hickey, editor of *The High-Tech Strategist,* a newsletter in Nashua, N.H.

Your best defense as an investor? Be extremely skeptical of the earnings announcements that companies make during the next few weeks. "News that a company beat its earnings estimates can't be taken as fact," warns Hickey. "What really matters," adds Charles David Scavone, a senior portfolio manager for AIM mutual funds, "is the quality of earnings, not the quantity."

Don't think that third-tier outfits are the only companies resorting to aggressive accounting strategies. Hewlett-Packard, for instance, handily beat consensus estimates when it reported its fiscal third-quarter earnings in an Aug. 16 press release, and CEO Carly Fiorini termed the results "superb." The company's stock price immediately jumped 10%. But the next day, HP shares gave back those gains amid concerns that the company had boosted profits with one-time gains and favorable currency and tax rates.

Fortunately, knowledge is power. The more you know about profit gimmicks, the better you'll be able to diagnose a company's financial health. Another plus: Comparing different companies will be easier when you know which ones are spin doctors and which play it straight. Here are some things to look out for.

■ **What you see is not what you get.** Companies sometimes tweak their earnings press releases to make profits look better than they are. For instance, companies increasingly highlight an earnings number that doesn't reflect all of their expenses. The real numbers—the ones calculated using generally accepted accounting principles (GAAP) that have to be reported to the Security & Exchange Commission—are usually listed at the end of the release and with little explanation or guidance. Companies defend the practice on the grounds that they're just pointing out what they feel is important in their results.

To spot these faux earnings, look for what are called pro forma results. Traditionally, companies use pro forma numbers only for an extraordinary event, like a merger or corporate restructuring, to show what earnings might have been had the event not occurred. But increasingly, technology companies are using pro forma earnings numbers that exclude certain items even when they aren't undergoing a transformation. "Pro forma numbers have their place, but some companies are taking advantage to make their earnings look better," says Charles Hill, director of research at First Call, which compiles and analyzes earnings and forecasts.

Hill says the practice began about two years ago when Yahoo! Inc. and other dot-coms began to exclude an expense called "goodwill" in pro forma earnings, and dubbed the reformulated number "cash earnings per share." Goodwill is an accounting term for the premium that an acquirer pays for another company that exceeds the fair market value of the acquired company's assets. Accounting rules require that goodwill be expensed, or amortized, over the lifetime of the acquired assets, up to 40 years. But because technology becomes obsolete so quickly, tech assets are usually amortized over a period of three to five years, which can result in hefty goodwill charges. Hill points out, for instance, that in Lycos' July quarter, it reported pro forma per-share earnings of 12¢, which excluded goodwill. If you add back the goodwill, the company had a loss of 36¢.

Hill says he counted more than 100 companies that excluded goodwill in the second-quarter earnings press releases. Indeed, the practice has become so widespread that the Financial Accounting Standards Board has proposed a rule that would require companies to report two earnings figures—one that includes the amortization of goodwill and one that doesn't.

That won't solve all the problems with pro forma earnings. Hill says about 100 additional companies ignore costs other than goodwill from their pro forma earnings. Most commonly, companies exclude the payroll taxes they owe when employees exercise stock options. For instance, in its second-quarter release, Qualcomm did not count as an expense the $12 million in payroll taxes it paid on exercised stock options. Another cost that companies ignore in pro formas are marketing expenses that are paid for with stock options or warrants.

To learn what the pro formas don't reveal, go directly to the GAAP numbers at the end of the earnings press release. You'll also want to check the Form 10-Qs that companies must file at the SEC within 45 days after the quarter's end. They're available—along with annual reports, proxies, and registration statements—at the EDGAR section of the SEC's Web site (www.sec.gov), or at Freedgar.com, whose more user-friendly software makes it easier to access the SEC database.

■ **Earnings don't matter.**
Another way that companies obscure actual earnings is to shift investor attention to EBITDA, or earnings before interest, taxes, depreciation, and amortization. For instance, in Exodus Communications' first-quarter earnings release, issued in April, CEO Ellen M. Hancock termed the results "a milestone" because the company had for the first time "achieved EBITDA profitability." However, Exodus, which manages Web sites for businesses, lost 32¢ a share that quarter.

EBITDA can be a legitimate measure of financial health for a company with long-lived assets, one that doesn't need to make much capital investment to keep the business going. The problem with many companies using EBITDA, says Pamela Stumpp, a senior vice-president at Moody's Investors Service, is that they generally must spend amounts equal to their depreciation to keep their equipment up-to-date.

■ **The options game.** Stock options have become a regular part of employees' compensation at many technology companies. But guess what. Current accounting rules don't require com-

panies to list stock-options grants as an expense in calculating earnings.

To determine the impact of options on a company's bottom line, you must look in the annual report for a footnote titled "diluted earnings per share." Although this footnote is rarely included in quarterly reports (Microsoft does so), thumbing through the footnotes in the last annual report will at least give you an idea of the impact of this maneuver in the previous year. Unfortunately, there is no way for investors to figure out the quarterly impact of such grants, says Pat McConnell, the chief accounting analyst at Bear Stearns. She argues that accounting rules should require companies to provide quarterly updates on stock options.

The hit to earnings can be substantial. Last year, Yahoo reported earnings of 10¢ a share. If the company had been forced to adjust its earnings for stock-options grants, Yahoo's profit would have turned into a 50¢-a-share loss, McConnell notes. Similarly, Autodesk's 16¢-a-share profit in 1999 would have instead been a 74¢ loss, she says. In a study of how stock-options grants affect the companies in the S&P 500, the analyst counted 21 companies in the index whose 1999 earnings would have fallen by 50% or more if stock-options grants were factored in. Technology and telecommunications companies were most likely to be impacted by stock-options grants, but they weren't the only ones. Gas- and oil-drillers, and some financial services and health-care companies also took big hits to earnings when stock-options grants were added to the equation, McConnell found.

Among the industry groups in the S&P 500 that were most affected, McConnell found that 1999 earnings at computer networking companies would have been 24% lower and 19% lower at telecommunications equipment makers. Because options are becoming such a popular way to pay employees, McConnell believes the impact of stock options grants on corporate America's bottom line will be even greater in the future.

■ **Boosting earnings with investment gains.** Many big technology companies such as Intel and Microsoft make venture-capital investments as part of their research-and-development efforts. If these venture-stage investments go public, the big companies can reap a bonanza: They suddenly have stock that can be sold at a profit when needed. "These investment gains are like a cookie jar," says David W. Tice, who runs the Prudent Bear Fund. "Companies can reach into it to make sure they make their earnings."

Indeed, these gains often give a big boost to a company's bottom line. For instance, when Microsoft reported its fiscal fourth-quarter earnings in July, it earned 44¢ a share and, as usual, beat Wall Street's expectations. But its reported earnings included a one-time investment gain of $1.1 billion, or 20¢ per share. Intel is another tech giant that has relied on big investment gains. For instance, the chip maker earned 50¢ a share in its June quarter, but 21¢ of that came from $1.5 billion in investment portfolio profits.

Big tech, telecom, and financial-services companies are most likely to have sizable investment portfolio gains. To find out what a company earned from investments, look at the "other income" figure on the profit-and-loss statement.

As the earnings season plays out, remember that the numbers the companies trumpet may not be the ones you really need to know. The critical numbers are there—you just have to dig them out.

Business Week
October 16, 2000
Pages 201 – 202 and 204

Questions for Consideration

1. Knowing that companies can use techniques to increase their earnings (and some do!), do you think that there is a loss of credibility in the financial statements?

2. Why would companies, such as Yahoo!, want to report pro forma earnings that exclude amortization of goodwill or depreciation expense, as well as other items?

Name _____ Professor _____

Course _____ Section _____

Assignment 9
Current Assets and Current Liabilities

Name of your company _____

This assignment focuses on the current asset and current liability sections of the balance sheet and the related notes to the financial statements. Upon completion, you should understand your company's holdings of current assets and current liabilities and how effectively your company is managing them.

Completing the assignment

1. Identify the changes in current asset and current liability accounts that occurred during the most recent accounting period.

Current Assets	Amount on Most Recent Balance Sheet	Amount at End of Prior Year	Net Change in Dollars	Net Change in Percent
Cash and cash equivalents	_____	_____	_____	_____
Temporary assets (or short-term investments, or short-term marketable securities)	_____	_____	_____	_____
Accounts receivable, net	_____	_____	_____	_____
Other receivables, net	_____	_____	_____	_____
Inventories	_____	_____	_____	_____
Deferred tax assets	_____	_____	_____	_____
Other _____	_____	_____	_____	_____
Other _____	_____	_____	_____	_____
Total current assets	_____	_____	_____	_____

These two numbers should match the numbers on the balance sheet.

(The assignment continues on the next page.)

Current Liabilities	Amount on Most Recent Balance Sheet	Amount at End of Prior Year	Net Change in Dollars	Net Change in Percent
Accounts payable	_____	_____	_____	_____
Short-term debt	_____	_____	_____	_____
Accrued salaries and wages	_____	_____	_____	_____
Deferred tax liabilities	_____	_____	_____	_____
Accrued interest	_____	_____	_____	_____
Current maturities of long-term debt	_____	_____	_____	_____
Other _____	_____	_____	_____	_____
Other _____	_____	_____	_____	_____
Other _____	_____	_____	_____	_____
Total current liabilities	=======	=======	=======	=====

These two numbers should match
the numbers on the balance sheet.

2. What significant changes (in amount or percentage) occurred during the most recent year among the current assets and current liabilities? Are any of the changes troubling? Are there any that you might want to investigate further if you were an owner or creditor of your firm? Discuss.

_____

_____

_____

_____

_____

_____

_____

_____

_____

3. Effective management of receivables is critical for most firms. Generally, the change in receivables should be consistent with the change in sales. Provide the following detailed information regarding sales, accounts receivable, and allowance for bad debts (also known as allowance for uncollectible accounts).

Hint: *Some of this detail may be listed in the notes to the financial statements.*

	End of Most Recent Year	End of Previous Year	Percent Change
a. Sales revenues	_____	_____	_____
b. Gross accounts receivable	_____	_____	_____
c. Less: Allowance for bad debts	_____	_____	_____
d. Net accounts receivable	_____	_____	_____
e. Allowance for bad debts as a percentage of sales	_____	_____	_____
f. Allowance for bad debts as a percentage of ending accounts receivable	_____	_____	_____

g. Are the percentage changes in accounts receivable and allowance for bad debts similar to the change in sales or are they different? Analyze and discuss the meaning or implications of any differences you observe.

_____

_____

_____

_____

_____

_____

_____

_____

_____

_____

_____

_____

4. Effective management of inventory is also critical for most firms. Changes in the levels of inventory should be consistent with changes in the level of cost of goods sold. For example, if the inventory balance increases sharply without a corresponding change in cost of goods sold, it may signal poor inventory management practices or sales expectations that did not materialize. Provide the following detailed information regarding cost of goods sold and the various categories of inventory.

Hint: *Some of this detail may be listed in the notes to the financial statements.*

> **Note**
>
> Not all firms have inventories. Companies that provide services instead of goods will not have meaningful amounts of inventory. For example, banks, insurance companies, electric power companies and airlines generally do not have meaningful amounts of inventory. As the United States moves to a more service-based economy, there are more and more companies such as Federal Express (package delivery services) and H&R Block (income tax preparation services) that do not have inventory.
>
> If your firm is primarily a service firm without significant amounts of inventory you may skip this section. Ask your professor if he/she wishes you to substitute another firm's data for this section of the assignment.

	End of Most Recent Year	End of Previous Year	Percent Change
a. Cost of goods sold	_____	_____	_____
b. Merchandise inventory	_____	_____	_____
c. Raw materials inventory	_____	_____	_____
d. Work in process inventory	_____	_____	_____
e. Finished goods inventory	_____	_____	_____
f. Other _____	_____	_____	_____
Total inventories	_____	_____	_____

sum of b, c, d, e, and f

g. Is the change in total inventories (and the change in each component of inventory) similar to the change in cost of goods sold or different? Discuss the implications of any differences you observe.

_____

_____

_____

_____

_____

_____

_____

_____

5. Which inventory valuation methods are used by your firm? (Mark all that apply.)

   Hint: *This information usually is provided in the first note to the financial statements. Service firms probably won't have inventories.*

   > **Note**
   > The Dollar-value LIFO, Retail LIFO, and Retail dollar-value LIFO methods listed below are merely specialized applications of the basic LIFO method you have learned about in class. In addition, almost every firm will report that they apply the lower-of-cost-or-market method. This means that the LIFO or FIFO amount does not exceed the cost of replacing the inventory. (As used here, "market" means replacement cost.)

   a. _____ Weighted average

   b. _____ FIFO

   c. _____ LIFO

   d. _____ Dollar-value LIFO

   e. _____ Retail LIFO

   f. _____ Retail dollar-value LIFO

   g. If more than one method is used, does one method predominate?

   _____ Yes   _____ No

   If so, indicate that method. _____

   h. Are inventories reported using lower-of-cost-or-market? _____

   > **Note**
   > The following four ratios provide information about how well a firm manages its current assets and current liabilities.
   >
   > **Current ratio** (also known as the **working capital ratio**) shows how many dollars of current assets are available to pay off each dollar of current liabilities (as of the balance sheet date). This ratio measures liquidity, the ability of a company to pay its bills as they come due.
   >
   > $$\frac{\text{current assets}}{\text{current liabilities}}$$
   >
   > **Quick ratio** (also known as the **acid-test ratio**) is a "tighter" measure of liquidity in that inventory and prepaid expenses are excluded from the numerator.
   >
   > $$\frac{\text{cash} + \text{cash equivalents} + \text{short} \cdot \text{term investments} + \text{accounts receivable}}{\text{current liabilities}}$$

Accounts receivable turnover ratio measures the velocity of receivables through the firm. In general, the faster that receivables are collected the better; the higher the turnover the better.

$$\frac{\text{sales revenue}}{\text{average accounts receivable}*}$$

Inventory turnover ratio is an indicator of how long inventory is held before being sold. A high turnover is favorable and means that inventory is held only a short time before sale.

$$\frac{\text{cost of goods sold}}{\text{average inventory}*}$$

$$* \frac{\text{beginning balance} + \text{ending balance}}{2}$$

6. Calculate each of the following ratios for the most recent year available. Enter your results into the first column of the table below. For perspective, compare your firm's ratios for the most recent year to those of your classmates' firms.

Alternative

As an alternative to comparing your company's ratios with those of your classmates' companies, you may want to compare with the companies you used in No. 3.e. of Assignment 5.

Check with your professor to make sure this option is acceptable.

	Your Firm	Firm 1	Firm 2	Firm 3	Firm 4	Firm 5
		C O M P A R A T I V E F I R M S				
a. Current ratio	___	___	___	___	___	___
b. Quick ratio (Acid-test ratio)	___	___	___	___	___	___
c. Accounts receivable turnover ratio	___	___	___	___	___	___
d. Inventory turnover ratio	___	___	___	___	___	___

7. How do your firm's ratios compare to those of your comparative firms? Are they high, low, or about the same? Is there anything specific about your firm, its industry, or your comparative firms or industries that might tend to explain the differences between your company's ratios and those of the other firms? Discuss.

_____

_____

_____

8. Optional Memo No. 2 – Current Assets and Current Liabilities

   Your second memo is based on what you have learned about your company's earnings and current accounts.

Guide for Memo No. 2

a. Having studied your company's income statement, discuss why you believe that your company is growing, declining, or remaining constant.

b. Perhaps the three most significant current accounts related to net income are accounts receivable, inventory, and accounts payable. Do the changes in these accounts appear consistent with your company's earnings pattern? Explain why or why not.

c. Based on this analysis of your company, would you add it to an equity portfolio?

   Explain.

Reading 9
A Thief Among Us

By William E. Grieshober
CPA, CIA, small business advisor for Buffalo State College, Buffalo, New York

Sometimes, even the most cautious investor can be deceived. But, with persistence and an auditor's edge, the truth can be unearthed.

Luke and Bert were partners in a $4 million sporting goods business. For the first 20 years, the business was very successful, but in the last three years, sales had decreased and margins dwindled. To help alleviate the decline in cash flow, the company's attorney suggested that the owners look for a third partner who could invest $200,000 and possibly add some management skills to complement the areas in which the others were weak.

Across town, Ed heard about the sporting-goods opportunity through an attorney in the law firm where he worked as an accountant and thought it sounded like exactly what he was looking for. But because Ed had once been an internal auditor, his instincts told him to analyze this opportunity in detail before investing.

Ed spent hours poring over the company's reports. Although there were no audited statements, Luke and Bert did have five years of financial information, including compilations and re-

views prepared by a certified public accounting firm. Ed was also given copies of the business' tax returns for the last four years. While reviewing the documents, he noticed that one of the company's largest assets was its inventory. When Ed met with the engagement partner of the CPA firm, he was assured that physical inventory tests were performed each year. Nevertheless, Ed asked for—and received—representation letters signed by both Luke and Bert attesting to the values of the inventory.

After completing due diligence, the sale closed two months before the company's fiscal year-end. Ed rolled up his sleeves and jumped into the business. He was working 60-plus hours every week trying to learn everything about the business as quickly as he could. He knew it would take all the energy he had to turn this business around, but he was willing to make the effort. Although Ed's expertise was in finance, Bert had been the company's chief accounting officer for 10 years and was reluctant to turn that role over to Ed. Not wanting to cause any problems, Ed concentrated on other areas such as human resources, training, and merchandising.

Even though he was not in charge of the books, Ed began to notice some alarming discrepancies. He first became troubled

when he realized that the company was inadequately prepared for its year-end inventory. No attempt had been made to relieve the general chaos of the merchandise; count sheets were used, but areas weren't straightened up and like-items weren't grouped together. The physical inventory began when the business closed and lasted until the final item was counted eight hours later. Every employee was expected to participate—at time and a half—and temporary employees were hired from an agency. During the recount phase, Ed found one section that had been missed with more than $3,000 worth of product and another section with several empty product boxes.

When the results of the inventory were tabulated, shrinkage was calculated at more than 20 percent of the total inventory of $975,000. That loss amounted to more than $200,000, which more than wiped out the investment that Ed had just made in the business, not to mention any profit for the year. Ed was not just uneasy; he was thoroughly confused.

Because Ed had been an auditor, he was well-equipped to investigate the problem. He drew up an audit program to reconcile the inventory. Choosing high-dollar items, he began reconstructing the inventory. He used the prior year's physical inventory report and traced purchases and sales in and out of the ware-house, reconciling each item to the report. One thing became evident early on—there were too many journal entries that showed increased physical unit counts at month-end.

Because Bert was in charge of the financial aspects of the business and ultimately responsible for journal entries, Ed discussed the discrepancies with Luke first. Luke disavowed any knowledge of the fictitious entries, so Ed went to the accounting clerk who made the entries. She told him that she was only acting upon Bert's instructions. According to her, Bert had falsified the inventory report so that it appeared to the bank as if there were enough merchandise to secure a loan. Whenever the inventory level fell below a certain amount, Bert "invented" some to cover the covenant amount. If a bank auditor came in to check, Bert had a supply of empty product boxes that he could put on the shelf. Apparently, the bank's auditor only counted boxes: He never opened or lifted any of them.

Finally, Ed confronted Bert with the evidential material that he had gathered. At first, Bert denied all knowledge of the fraud. But because Ed had the facts to back up his assertions, Bert confessed that not only had

he falsified the inventory, he'd been doing it for a number of years. Bert admitted that the company had not been profitable for more than six years, and he had been falsifying inventory so it looked as though there was moderate income. It started because the company had a one-year loss of around $30,000 and Bert was afraid that the bank would close them down. He began fabricating inventory, always thinking that the company would be able to make it up the next year, which of course, never happened.

Because Bert had intentionally defrauded the new partner, Ed had Bert sign a waiver of rights against the company and its officers. Ed also asked for and received Bert's resignation. Although he was unable to prove that the CPA firm was involved in the commission of the fraud, Ed had his suspicions. At best, the firm was negligent in the observation of the physical inventory. Ed discussed the problem with the firm's engagement partner, and received the company's withdrawal from the engagement as well as a refund of all monies paid them during the last two years.

When Ed talked to the bank's officials, they chose to change the covenants and allow Ed and

Luke to work out the loan over an extended period of time rather than close the business and suffer the loss. The two new partners continued to run the business in a declining marketplace, but they were able to turn it around through cost-cutting measures.

Eventually, Ed and Luke had an opportunity to sell the business. Ed recovered his investment and Luke finally received some of his investment, too.

LESSONS LEARNED

- If top management is unprincipled, it is very difficult to conduct due diligence.
- Audit tools are useful even to managers.
- Cursory inventory observations are next to worthless. Boxes must be opened and product examined to ensure it matches the description.
- If something makes you uncomfortable, don't hesitate to investigate further.
- Make sure you have all the facts before confronting someone you suspect of falsifying information.
- Fraud perpetrators and those involved with a fraud may provide restitution.

Internal Auditor
December 2000
Pages 71 and 73

Questions for Consideration

1. What effect(s) does overstating ending inventory have on a company's financial statements?

2. Could this inventory fraud have been executed without the cooperation of the accounting clerk?

Assignment 10
Long-term Assets

Name of your company _____

In this assignment you will review and evaluate the decisions which your company's management has made regarding long-term assets. This includes plant (or fixed) assets, intangible assets, and long-term investments.

Completing the Assignment

1. Identify the changes in your firm's long-term asset accounts that occurred during the most recent accounting period. You will probably have to search the footnotes to obtain some of the specific account information requested. Blank spaces have been provided for you to write in any additional items that appear in your company's Annual Report or SEC 10-K under long-term assets.

Long-term Assets	Amount on Most Recent Balance Sheet	Amount at End of Prior Year	Net Change in Dollars	in Percent
Machinery and equipment	_____	_____	_____	_____
Building (and leasehold improvements)	_____	_____	_____	_____
Land	_____	_____	_____	_____
Other _____	_____	_____	_____	_____
Other _____	_____	_____	_____	_____
Other _____	_____	_____	_____	_____
Less: Accumulated depreciation	_____	_____	_____	_____
Net* Property, Plant and Equipment	_____	_____	_____	_____
Construction in progress	_____	_____	_____	_____
Deferred tax assets	_____	_____	_____	_____
Long-term receivables	_____	_____	_____	_____

*Original cost of depreciable assets minus accumulated depreciation to date.

Long-term Assets (cont.)	Amount on Most Recent Balance Sheet	Amount at End of Prior Year	Net Change in Dollars	in Percent
Long-term investments	_____	_____	_____	_____
Excess of cost over net assets of acquired companies, i.e., goodwill	_____	_____	_____	_____
Patents, copyrights, and trademarks	_____	_____	_____	_____
Other _____	_____	_____	_____	_____
Other _____	_____	_____	_____	_____
Total long-term assets	_____	_____	_____	_____

These two numbers should match
the numbers on the balance sheet.

2. Based on the information above, briefly summarize the significant changes in long-term asset accounts, if any, that occurred during the most recent year.

_____

_____

_____

_____

_____

_____

_____

_____

_____

_____

_____

_____

_____

_____

_____

3. Accounting policies related to long-term assets

Hint: Most of this information will be found in the first note to the financial statements.

> **Note**
>
> The terms depreciation, amortization, and depletion are used to indicate very similar processes. All refer to the process of allocating part of the cost of a long-term asset to expense.
>
> ▸ When allocating a portion of the cost of tangible fixed assets to expense, accountants use the term *depreciation*.
>
> ▸ When referring to this process for intangible assets, accountants use the term *amortization*.
>
> ▸ When referring to this process for natural resource assets, accountants use the term *depletion*.

a. Depreciation: Which depreciation method(s) does your firm use for financial reporting purposes? Check all that apply.

   1) _____   Straight-line

   2) _____   Sum-of-the-year's digits

   3) _____   Declining-balance

   4) _____   Other (specify) _____

   5) If multiple depreciation methods are used, which method is used predominantly? _____

   6) Does your firm disclose the estimated useful lives that it assumes for depreciating its tangible fixed assets. If yes, describe them.

   _____

   _____

   _____

b. Does your firm report any intangible assets on the balance sheet? If yes, describe the policies, e.g., method and estimated life, your firm uses to compute amortization expense.

   _____

   _____

   _____

c. Does your firm report any natural resource assets? If yes, describe the policies, e.g., method and estimated useful life, your firm uses to compute depletion expense.

   _____

   _____

   _____

> **Note**
>
> When one firm controls another firm (such as by owning more than 50% of its voting stock), the second firm is a subsidiary of the first and *consolidated* financial statements are presented.
>
> Consolidated statements combine the financial information of the subsidiaries with that of the parent firm. Use of the term "consolidated" in the title of financial statements indicates that the firm controls at least one other firm.

4. Does your firm own one or more subsidiaries?

_____ Yes   _____ No

Hint: *Does your firm present "consolidated" financial statements, e.g., consolidated balance sheet, consolidated income statement?*

a. If the answer to No. 4 was yes, determine whether all the subsidiaries are 100% wholly-owned.

   Hint: *If any subsidiary is only partially owned, there will be an account listed on the balance sheet (usually after long-term liabilities but before stockholders' equity) with a title something like "Minority Interest." Check one of the following.*

   1) _____ All subsidiaries are 100% wholly-owned.

   2) _____ At least one subsidiary is less than 100% wholly-owned.

> **Note**
>
> In general, when a company owns stock of another firm, but not enough to control the firm, this ownership of shares is accounted for as an "investment" and is reported under long-term assets on the investor company's balance sheet.

b. Did your firm report any investments in other firms on its balance sheet under the category of long-term investments?

   _____ Yes   _____ No

c. If yes, inspect the notes to the financial statements to determine which of the following accounting methods are used by your firm to account for this investment(s). Mark all of the following that apply.

   1) _____ Cost method

   2) _____ Market-to-market (or fair value) method

   3) _____ Equity method

d. Did your firm acquire or dispose of any subsidiaries or investments in other firms during the most recent year?

Hint: *This will be discussed in the notes if it occurred. It will probably also show up on the statement of cash flows.*

If yes, describe the acquisitions or disposals that occurred.

_____

_____

_____

_____

_____

_____

_____

_____

_____

_____

_____

_____

Note

The following four ratios provide information about a company's use of long-term assets.

Depreciation and amortization to average long-term assets ratio indicates how rapidly the firm is expensing (writing off) its long-term assets. This can be critical in an industry experiencing rapidly changing technology.

$$\frac{\text{depreciation expense } + \text{ amortization expense}}{\text{average long} \cdot \text{term assets}^*}$$

$$^*\frac{\text{current year' s ending balance } + \text{ prior year' s ending balance}}{2}$$

Long-term assets to total assets ratio indicates a firm's financial flexibility. The larger the portion of long-term assets, the less flexibility the firm has to change strategies quickly.

$$\frac{\text{long} \cdot \text{term assets}}{\text{total assets}}$$

Plant assets to total assets ratio indicates financial flexibility but focuses only on the investment in land, buildings, equipment, etc.

$$\frac{\text{plant assets}}{\text{total assets}}$$

Sales to average plant assets ratio measures productivity of the plant assets. It shows how many dollars of sales were generated by each dollar invested in plant assets. (How hard are the plant assets working?)

$$\frac{\text{sales}}{\text{average plant assets*}}$$

$$* \; \frac{\text{beginning balance} \; + \; \text{ending balance}}{2}$$

5. Compute each of the four ratios above for the most recent year and enter the result in the first column below. To give perspective to your results, check with five classmates to determine the value of the ratios for their firms. Record the information below.

Alternative

As an alternative to comparing your company's ratios with those of your classmates' companies, you may want to compare with the companies you used in No. 3.e. of Assignment 5.

Check with your professor to make sure this alternative is acceptable.

	Your Firm	COMPARATIVE FIRMS				
		Firm 1	Firm 2	Firm 3	Firm 4	Firm 5
a. $\dfrac{\text{deprec. exp.} + \text{amort. exp.}}{\text{average long-term assets}}$	_____	_____	_____	_____	_____	_____
b. $\dfrac{\text{long-term assets}}{\text{total assets}}$	_____	_____	_____	_____	_____	_____
c. $\dfrac{\text{plant assets}}{\text{total assets}}$	_____	_____	_____	_____	_____	_____
d. $\dfrac{\text{sales}}{\text{average plant assets}}$	_____	_____	_____	_____	_____	_____

e. How do your firm's long-term asset ratios compare to those of your comparison firms? Are they high, low, about the same? Is there anything specific about your firm, its industry, or your comparison firms or industries that tend to explain the differences between your company's long-term asset ratios and those of the other firms?

Discuss and explain.

_____

_____

_____

_____

_____

_____

_____

_____

_____

_____

_____

_____

_____

_____

_____

_____

_____

_____

_____

_____

_____

_____

_____

_____

_____

_____

Reading 10
Goodwill Hunting: Accounting Change May Lift Profits, But Stock Prices May Not Follow Suit

By Jonathan Weil
The Wall Street Journal Staff Reporter

If you think perception is more important than reality, some Wall Street analysts may have just the right stock-picking strategy for you.

It has to do with an intangible asset called goodwill and a new proposal by the nation's accounting-rule makers that would change the way companies treat goodwill on their financial statements. Goodwill is the difference between the purchase price paid for an acquisition and the fair value of the acquired company's net assets. And for companies with a lot of goodwill on their balance sheets, it has long been a big drag on earnings.

Current accounting rules require companies to steadily write down their goodwill assets over periods as long as 40 years, expensing the charges against earnings along the way. But that likely will change later this year. Under a proposal that was affirmed yesterday by the Financial Accounting Standards Board, companies no longer would gradually write down their goodwill. Instead, they would let goodwill sit untouched on their balance sheets until the value becomes impaired, at which point they would be required to write some or even all of it off.

Consequently, many compa-

nies active on the acquisition front will see their earnings boosted when the incremental drag from goodwill amortization goes away. And higher earnings mean higher stock prices, right?

That's how some analysts are calling it, anyway. For instance, in a research note last month on electronics conglomerate **Tyco International**, Merrill Lynch analyst Phua Young wrote that Tyco's earnings for fiscal 2001, which ends in September, could be close to $3 a share if the FASB proposal goes through, compared with his current $2.70 estimate. "In our view, the shares of Tyco International were inexpensive before this proposal," Mr. Young wrote. "However, the new FASB would make the shares even more attractive... ."

Of course, there's a glitch in this school of thought, which even proponents such as Mr. Young concede: It's illogical. After all, whether or not a company amortizes its goodwill has nothing to do with how much its business is intrinsically worth. Goodwill is, purely and simply, a bookkeeping item, with no connection to cash flow, and many savvy investors long have ignored goodwill charges in evaluating what a stock is worth.

So Mr. Young's analysis that Tyco shares will look more attractive under the new account-

ing treatment is about psychology: It plays off the observation that many investors are fixated on companies' bottom-line numbers with little concern for how they're tabulated, and that they often plug these numbers into price-to-earnings equations (one of the most simplistic methods around for valuing a stock) in a color-by-numbers fashion.

Goodwill bulls believe that most companies' stocks will continue to trade at their current price-to-earnings ratios even after the FASB proposal takes effect, though in a rational world, critics respond, these ratios should fall. And even if an investor doesn't believe the accounting change should boost stock prices, the thinking goes, he or she should act on the belief that others think it will.

Take, for example, a company that has earnings of $1 a share and a stock price of $10 before the rule change. Now assume its earnings jump to $1.20 because the company no longer is amortizing goodwill. The goodwill bulls say they expect the market to still value the stock at 10 times earnings, resulting in a $12 stock.

"It makes no economic sense," says Trevor Harris, an accounting expert at Morgan Stanley Dean Witter, who says he has tried to discourage analysts at his firm from using such arguments to tout the stocks they cover. "There should be no long-term price effect. And if there is any initial price effect, it's purely a momentum play that has no duration."

In the wake of the proposal, Mr. Young is hardly alone in identifying stocks whose earnings would be higher under the accounting-rule change. At UBS Warburg, chief strategist Edward Kerschner this week issued a report recommending 10 companies that he described as beneficiaries of the accounting change. Among them: **International Paper**, **Pepsi Bottling Group** and tech stocks **PerkinElmer** and **Thermo Electron**.

By UBS's projections, these companies' earnings estimates for 2001 would be around 20% to 30% higher if the FASB proposal goes through. And earnings for companies in the Standard & Poor's 500-stock index should get an aggregate boost of 5% to 6%, though Mr. Kerschner notes that lower earnings quality also will be a result, "because the increase in earnings represents just an accounting change, not an economic change."

"In theory, this has no economic impact," Mr. Kerschner says. "But certainly on the margins, this has to make some stocks look more attractive."

Lehman Brothers analyst Robert Cornell, who follows electrical-equipment makers, estimates that **General Electric**'s 2000 earnings would be 13% higher without goodwill amortization, while **SPX**'s 2000 earnings would be 19% higher. As a result, he expects to raise his price targets on those stocks and others, believing their price-to-earnings ratios will stay constant as their earnings benefit from the absence of goodwill amortization.

"It's intellectually indefensible that the [price-to-earnings] multiples will stay the same," Mr. Cornell says. "But I think the reality is that the market isn't perfectly efficient in that regard, and it will reflect what it's been told to look at. And that is earnings per share."

Messrs. Cornell and Kerschner caution investors not to take this approach to extremes. For instance, if a company's earnings double because of the FASB proposal, Mr. Cornell says the market likely won't blindly keep the same price-to-earnings multiple on its stock. Also, the rule change should have no impact on the stock prices of companies (including many profitless ones) that long ago persuaded analysts and investors to ignore their official bottom-line numbers and to focus instead on alternative earnings measures that exclude such expenses as depreciation and amortization.

Further, Mr. Kerschner cautions that many companies inevitably will have to take large impairment charges to earnings because their goodwill assets are excessively valued. Given that they're bookkeeping entries that don't affect the operations of a company, big impairment charges alone wouldn't force companies into financial difficulties, even if the result is negative shareholder equity. But the charges would amount to confessions of how much money com-

panies had wasted on poor acquisitions in the past. "If you see a company that's impairing every 12 to 18 months, it might be a statement about management's ability," Mr. Kerschner says.

According to a study released this month by accounting professors Steven Henning and Wayne Shaw of Southern Methodist University in Dallas, there has been no relation historically between companies' stock prices and goodwill-amortization charges. And that suggests that the elimination of goodwill amortization should have little, if any, impact on companies' market values. "It shouldn't matter from a rational standpoint," Mr. Shaw says.

As for Mr. Young, the Merrill analyst, he's sticking to his FASB-related call on Tyco, based on the conclusion that Tyco's fiscal 2001 earnings would be roughly 10% higher without goodwill amortization. "If you add back that 10%, that stock is now that much less expensive, or even more undervalued, depending on your perspective," he says. "It's just the perception. That's nine-tenths of the game."

Traditionalists counter that investors are better off sticking with fundamentals, rather than trying to predict what other investors' future misconceptions might be. "I would hope that people read behind the numbers," says Steven Lilien, chairman of the accounting department at Baruch College in New York. "I'd have to believe they do. Otherwise, you could create wealth simply through accounting changes."

Goodwill Gains

Under a new accounting-rule proposal, companies no longer would amortize goodwill assets. This would provide a big boost to many companies' future earnings, although it theoretically should have no impact on stock prices, because it simply reflects a bookkeeping change. Here's a look at the potential earnings increases for some companies, according to a Jan. 21 report by UBS Warburg.

Company	Yesterday's closing share price	Earnings-per-share estimate for 2001		
		Under current rules	Assuming no goodwill amortization	% change
CIT Group	$21.75	$2.52	$2.87	14%
International Paper	36.25	2.00	2.41	21
Johnson Controls	62.94	5.45	6.34	16
Pepsi Bottling Group	37.38	1.77	2.30	30
PerkinElmer	86.00	2.31	3.05	32
Thermo Electron	27.55	0.78	1.00	28

Sources: All earnings estimates are by UBS Warburg analysts

The Wall Street Journal
January 25, 2001
Pages C1 – C2

Questions for Consideration

1. Analysts appear to hold differing views on the effect of the proposed goodwill accounting standard. Discuss the range of effects possible.

2. Do you think that investors will "see through" the effects of the proposed accounting standard on goodwill?

Assignment 11
Long-term Liabilities

Name of your company _____

The purpose of this assignment is to understand and evaluate the decisions your company's management has made regarding long-term liabilities.

Key References for this Assignment

1. *Mergent Bond Record*, Mergent FIS, Inc. (a monthly service), formerly *Moody's Bond Record*, Moody's Investors Service, or

2. *Standard and Poor's Bond Guide*, Standard & Poor's, Inc. (a monthly service)

Completing the Assignment

1. Identify the changes in the long-term liability accounts that occurred during the most recent accounting period. Blank spaces have been provided for you to write in additional items that appear in your firm's long-term liability section.

Long-term Liabilities	Amount on Most Recent Balance Sheet	Amount at End of Prior Year	Net Change in Dollars	in Percent
Long-term debt	_____	_____	_____	_____
Capitalized lease obligations	_____	_____	_____	_____
Deferred tax liabilities	_____	_____	_____	_____
Pension liability	_____	_____	_____	_____
Other _____	_____	_____	_____	_____
Total long-term liabilities	_____	_____	_____	_____

These two numbers should match the numbers on the balance sheet.

2. Based on the information in No. 1 and that found in the notes to the financial statements, briefly summarize the significant changes, if any, in the long-term liability accounts during the most recent year.

_____

_____

_____

_____

_____

_____

_____

_____

_____

_____

_____

_____

3. What are the approximate interest rates incurred on your firm's long-term liabilities? Complete the schedule below. Some items, e.g., deferred tax liabilities, do not incur interest. Some (or most) of this information will be found in the notes to the financial statements.

Long-term Liability Accounts   **Approximate Rate of Interest**

_____   _____ %

_____   _____ %

_____   _____ %

_____   _____ %

_____   _____ %

_____   _____ %

4. What amount of cash is the firm obligated to pay out in each of the next five years for repayment of long-term debt, capitalized lease obligations, operating leases, and/or other commitments?

    Hint: _This information usually is contained in the notes to the financial statements and will take careful reading to identify._

Year	Repayment of Long-term Debt	Capital Lease Obligations	Operating Leases	Other Commitments
Year 1	_____	_____	_____	_____
Year 2	_____	_____	_____	_____
Year 3	_____	_____	_____	_____
Year 4	_____	_____	_____	_____
Year 5	_____	_____	_____	_____
Totals	_____	_____	_____	_____

5. Go to the statement of cash flows. Observe the amount of "net cash flow from operations" generated in each of the last three years. To what extent does it appear that the company will be able to pay off the above scheduled obligations each year with cash generated from operations? Might the company need to raise the required cash in some other way? Discuss.

6. Find and read the footnote about your firm's pension plan(s). Then answer the following questions.

    a. Which type(s) of pension plan does your firm have? Check all that apply. The firm may have either type of plan, both, or none.

        _____ Defined contribution plan

        _____ Defined benefit plan

        _____ None

    b. Fill in the blanks below to determine if your company has sufficient assets to satisfy its pension obligations.

        1) Fair value of pension plan assets   _____

            Less: accumulated benefit obligation (ABO)   – _____

            Excess (deficiency) of plan assets over ABO   = _____

        2) Fair value of pension plan assets   _____

            Less: projected benefit obligation (PBO)   – _____

            Excess (deficiency) of plan assets over PBO   = _____

> **Note**
>
> The accumulated benefit obligation (ABO) is the present value of all pension benefits that employees have earned to date based on their *current* wage rates.
>
> The projected benefit obligation (PBO) is the present value of all pension benefits that employees have earned to date based on their *expected* wage rates at the time they retire.

c. If the company were liquidated today, would there be enough pension plan assets for the firm to meet its obligations to its employees? Explain.

   Hint: *Focus on the ABO.*

   _____

   _____

   _____

   _____

   _____

d. If you acquired the company and its employees today, are there enough pension plan assets to cover benefits earned-to-date when the employees retire at their normal retirement dates? Explain.

   Hint: *Focus on the PBO.*

   _____

   _____

   _____

   _____

   _____

7. Identify the investment characteristics of your firm's long-term debt. Obtain the most recent monthly issue of either *Mergent* (formerly *Moody's*) *Bond Record* or *Standard & Poor's Bond Guide*. (Companies are listed alphabetically in both publications, but if you have a choice, *Mergent Bond Record* is a little easier to use.) Look up your company to determine whether it has any long-term debt listed, and if so, answer each of the following questions. (If your firm has more than three issues, select three representative issues for listing here.)

	Long-term Debt Issue #1	**Long-term Debt Issue #2**	**Long-term Debt Issue #3**
a. Type of debt (Notes, subordinated notes, senior notes, debentures, etc.)	_____	_____	_____
b. Interest rate	_____	_____	_____
c. Year debt is due	_____	_____	_____
d. Debt rating (indicate which rating source you used)			
_____ Mergent	_____	_____	_____
_____ S&P	_____	_____	_____

e. Indicate whether the issue is "investment grade" (rated Baa/BBB or higher) or "speculative grade" ("junk bonds").

	Long-term Debt Issue #1	**Long-term Debt Issue #2**	**Long-term Debt Issue #3**
	_____	_____	_____

If your company has no bonds rated by Mergent/Moody's or S&P, skip to No. 8.

f. Call date of the debt, if any   _____   _____   _____

g. Call price of the debt, if any   _____   _____   _____

h. Current market price   _____   _____   _____

i. Recent price range

    Highest price   _____   _____   _____

    Lowest price   _____   _____   _____

j. Yield to maturity   _____   _____   _____

8. Did your firm disclose any contingencies, sometimes called contingent liabilities, in the notes to the financial statements? Discuss the specific nature of these contingencies and how (or whether) they are expected to affect the firm's financial health.

_____

_____

_____

_____

_____

_____

_____

_____

_____

_____

_____

_____

_____

> **Note**
> The following two ratios are computed to provide information about how a company is managing its long-term liabilities.
>
> **Debt to total assets ratio** reveals the percentage of assets financed by debt. The use of debt financing is referred to as financial leverage. The higher the degree of financial leverage, the higher the risk that a company will not be able to meet its interest payments and will be forced into bankruptcy.
>
> $$\frac{\text{total liabilities}}{\text{total assets}}$$
>
> **Times interest earned ratio** measures the cushion a company has regarding its ability to pay interest charges on its debt. The higher the cushion, the more likely the company will be able to meet its interest payments.
>
> $$\frac{*\text{net income} + [\text{interest expense} (1 - \text{tax rate})]}{\text{interest expense}}$$
>
> *Many companies report a number on the income statement using the title *operating income*. This amount is often used in the numerator of this ratio instead of the more complex computation shown above. If your company reports *operating income*, use it in the numerator of this ratio.

9. Calculate each of the following ratios for the most recent year using the computational formulas just explained.

   a. Debt to total assets $= \dfrac{\text{total liabilities}}{\text{total assets}}$

   Debt to total assets $= \underline{\hspace{5cm}} = \underline{\hspace{2cm}}\%$

   b. Times interest earned $= \dfrac{\text{net income} + [\text{interest expense} (1 - \text{tax rate})]}{\text{interest expense}}$

   Times interest earned $= \underline{\hspace{6cm}} = \underline{\hspace{2cm}}$

10. Enter your results into the first column of the table on the next page. For perspective, compare your firm's ratios for the most recent year to those of your classmates' firms.

Alternative

As an alternative to comparing your company's ratios to those of your classmates' companies, you may want to compare with the companies you used in

No. 3.e. of Assignment 5.

Check with your professor to make sure this option is acceptable.

	Your Firm	COMPARATIVE FIRMS				
		Firm 1	Firm 2	Firm 3	Firm 4	Firm 5
a. Debt to total assets	_____	_____	_____	_____	_____	_____
b. Times interest earned	_____	_____	_____	_____	_____	_____

11. How do your firm's ratios compare to those of your comparative firms? Are they high, low, about the same? Is there anything specific about your firm, its industry, or your comparative firms or industries that might tend to explain the differences between your company's ratios and those of the other firms? Discuss.

_____

_____

_____

_____

_____

_____

_____

_____

_____

_____

_____

_____

_____

_____

_____

_____

_____

_____

_____

_____

_____

_____

_____
_____
_____
_____
_____
_____
_____
_____
_____
_____
_____

Reading 11
Corporate Money Managers Begin to Get Some Respect

Reprinted with permission of *The Wall Street Journal*. Permission conveyed through Copyright Clearance Center, Inc.

By Gregory Zuckerman
The Wall Street Journal Staff Reporter

Deals & Deal Makers

The market focuses on acquisitions and new products, one official says, 'but AT&T can save hundreds of millions of dollars over the life of its bond issue and people don't appreciate that.'

At a family gathering this year, Sean Lannan was asked by his wife's cousin what he did for a living. Mr. Lannan, who works for telecommunications giant Lucent Technologies Inc., answered with pride: "I'm the director of capital markets at Lucent."

Uncomfortable silence. Blank stares. The conversation quickly shifted to the weather. "People always think the title sounds important, but they don't know what I actually do," says Mr. Lannan.

Mr. Lannan and other executives who decide when companies should sell bonds to investors, and how much they should sell, will never be the life of the party in the real world. But in corporate America, and to an extent on Wall Street, they're increasingly getting respect.

That's because the bond market has been as tough on the nerves as a fourth cup of coffee,

and executives who guessed right and sold a ton of bonds at just the right time saved their companies hundreds of millions of dollars.

Consider AT&T Corp.'s decision in March to sell $8 billion of bonds, shattering the record for the biggest bond deal on record. Some on Wall Street questioned the wisdom of raising so much money then, after interest rates had already moved higher. But rates have continued to climb, and the move now looks like a savvy one: If AT&T were to sell the same amount of bonds today it would have to pay $86 million a year more in interest payments over the next 30 years, a whopping $680 million in today's dollars.

Lucent itself sold $1.4 billion of bonds at a yield of 6.50% in March, after Mr. Lannan's team, together with Chief Financial Officer Don Pederson, determined that the economy would keep growing, forcing the Federal Reserve to raise interest rates to keep inflation at bay.

The Fed proceeded to raise interest rates three times this year, and bond investors have gone through periods in which they fled from all kinds of bonds, including Lucent's. In fact, to get the same deal done today, the company would have to pay investors a yield of about 7.20%

on its bonds, meaning Lucent saved about $11 million a year for the next 30 years, or about $138 million in today's dollars.

Treasurers, directors of capital markets and even chief financial officers often make these gutsy bets and can save their companies piles of money. But while chief executive officers get lots of credit for savvy strategic decisions, and many are even household names—think Michael Eisner, Bill Gates and John Welch—finance executives are often only recognized within their own households.

"It's not as bad as being a proctologist, but it's right up there," says Mr. Pederson of Lucent. Capital-raising is "taken for granted if it's done well, but if we screw up everyone knows about it."

To be sure, a growing number of chief financial officers have made a name for themselves and gone on to high-profile jobs, heading or helping to run companies. Douglas Ivester was the CFO of Coca-Cola Co. before eventually becoming chief executive. Jerome York was the chief financial officer of Chrysler Corp. and International Business Machines Corp. before leaving to become vice chairman of Kirk Kerkorian's Tracinda Corp.

And thanks in part to savvy financing moves, Daniel E.

Somers, AT&T's chief financial officer at the time of its bond deal, last week was named president and chief executive of AT&T Broadband & Internet Services, which manages the company's cable initiatives. Some even see him as a possible successor of AT&T Chairman Michael Armstrong.

To executives charged with running capital-raising efforts, the stakes are high. "I live and die on these decisions," Mr. Somers said in an interview earlier this year, noting that his boss, Mr. Armstrong, encouraged AT&T's decision to jump into the bond market.

Roy Guthrie, chief financial officer at Associates First Capital Corp., says: "In my chair, you sweat" having to decide when to issue bonds and how much to sell.

Mr. Guthrie should know. He says some investment bankers second-guessed Associates' decision to sell $7.3 billion of fixed-rate bonds between October 1998 and June of this year. But the company has saved $77 million a year over 20 years, $383 million in today's dollars, by acting before rates jumped and investors turned lukewarm to corporate bonds.

"Many companies got caught by paying up for financing in the third quarter but we didn't have to," he says.

Companies with heavy financing needs that go to the bond market regularly don't have the luxury of timing the bond market. They usually pay Wall Street firms to swap their interest-rate payments for floating-rate payments that move with interest rates. But companies without pressing needs can be choosier. Finance executives like Mr. Lannan gather intelligence on the future of rates, polling investors, Wall Street traders and analysts, with the goal of getting to the bond market when bonds are selling like hotcakes, and yields are low, rather than hot potatoes.

"We're involved in various parts of the economy so we have a view" of the future of interest rates, says Scott McCarthy, senior vice president of capital markets at Associates.

The task is crucial, Wall Street analysts say. The stock market tends to focus on high-profile acquisitions and new-product announcements, says Blake Bath of Lehman Brothers, "but AT&T can save hundreds of millions of dollars

over the life of its bond issue and people don't appreciate that."

So what should companies eager to raise money do now? Head for the bond market, say top financing executives. The economy shows few signs of slowing and the Fed may have to raise rates several times next year to keep inflation under wraps. Unless you can wait until the economy slows, perhaps during the second half of the year, sell your bonds now.

"Rates are heading higher and we see several more Fed [rate increases] in the cards," says Mr. Lannan of Lucent. "There's good demand from investors right now" so companies should sell bonds now, rather than later.

Adds Mr. Guthrie of Associates: "Pricing power will manifest itself in inflationary biases" in the next year, forcing the Fed to raise interest rates and the yield on the 30-year Treasury bond above 6.50%.

Associates is set to follow its own advice. "We're going to be pretty aggressive out of the gate in year 2000 about raising money," says Mr. Guthrie.

The Wall Street Journal
December 14, 1999
Pages C1 and C30

Questions for Consideration

1. Assume that both the stated and yield interest rate in March, 1999, are 6.5%. Would the Lucent bonds have sold at a discount, premium or at par? Why? Verify that Lucent would save $11 million per year in cash paid for interest.

2. Why is it important for a company to properly time a debt issue?

Name _____   Professor _____

Course _____   Section _____

Assignment 12
Stockholders' Equity

Name of your company _____

When you have completed this assignment, you should have a thorough understanding of the equity financing activities that your company has engaged in, both
during the current period and over its life. Use the information in your firm's
annual report to Stockholders and its SEC 10-K Report to complete this assignment. In addition, you will need to consult the most recent issue of *The Wall Street
Journal* or the Sunday edition of your local newspaper.

Completing the Assignment

1. Identify the categories and amounts of your firm's capital stock. Some companies have more than one class of common stock, e.g., Class A common and
   Class B common. Similarly, some companies have more than one issue of
   preferred stock. Complete the following table for each class of your firm's
   common stock and each class of your firm's preferred stock. Clearly identify
   each class of stock and indicate the number of shares in 000's.

Common stock	Authorized	Issued	Outstanding	Par Value (or Stated Value) Per Share
_____	_____	_____	_____	_____
_____	_____	_____	_____	_____
_____	_____	_____	_____	_____

Preferred stock (if any)

_____	_____	_____	_____	_____
_____	_____	_____	_____	_____
_____	_____	_____	_____	_____

2. Identify the changes in your firm's equity accounts that occurred during the
   most recent accounting period. Not all firms will have an entry for each item
   while some companies will have items that are not listed here.

Equity accounts	Amount on Most Recent Balance Sheet	Amount at End of Prior Year	Net Change in Dollars	Net Change in Percent
Preferred stock	_____	_____	_____	_____
Common stock	_____	_____	_____	_____
Additional paid-in capital (excess over par)	_____	_____	_____	_____
Deferred compensation	_____	_____	_____	_____
Cumulative translation adjustments	_____	_____	_____	_____
Retained earnings	_____	_____	_____	_____
Treasury stock	_____	_____	_____	_____
Other _____	_____	_____	_____	_____
Total stockholders' equity	=========	=========	========	=====

These two numbers should match
the totals on the balance sheet.

3. Briefly summarize the *significant* changes in stockholders' equity, if any, that occurred during the most recent year.

_____

_____

_____

_____

_____

_____

_____

4. _____ Check here if your firm had no preferred stock outstanding.

If your company had preferred stock outstanding at any time during the most recent year, indicate which of the following features apply.

   Yes   No

a. _____   _____   Cumulative

b. _____   _____   Participating

c. _____   _____   Redeemable

d. _____   _____   Convertible

e. _____   _____   Voting privileges

f. For characteristics a. through e. that apply to your firm's preferred stock, indicate the specifics of that characteristic to your stock. For example, if it is convertible, under what terms can it be converted?

Hint: Most of this information will be in the notes.

_____

_____

_____

_____

_____

_____

_____

5. Indicate below whether your firm had treasury stock at the end of the current period and/or at the end of the prior period.

	Current Balance Sheet	Prior Balance Sheet	Percent Change
a. Number of shares	_____	_____	_____
b. Dollar amount	_____	_____	_____
c. Is it reported at its cost? (If not, ignore d.)	_____	_____	_____
d. What was the average price* paid to acquire the treasury stock?	_____	_____	_____

$$* \text{ average price } = \frac{\text{total cost}}{\text{number of shares}}$$

6. Did your company issue stock, either common or preferred, during the most recent year?

Hint: This is reported on the statement of stockholders' equity if one is included in the financial statements. Otherwise, look on the statement of cash flows under Financing Activities and/or on a supplementary schedule that sometimes accompanies the statement of cash flows.

_____ Yes

_____ No

If yes, identify the number of shares issued of each type of stock, par value (if any), and total dollar amount received from each issue.

Type of Stock	Number of Shares Issued	Par Value (Per Share)	Total Dollar Amount
a. _____	_____	_____	_____
b. _____	_____	_____	_____
c. _____	_____	_____	_____
d. _____	_____	_____	_____

7. Does your firm have any executive stock options outstanding at its most recent balance sheet date?

_____

If yes, by what percent would the number of common shares outstanding increase if all executive stock options were exercised? Show your clearly labeled work in the space provided below.

_____ %

Note

The following three ratios are computed to provide information about a company's common stock price and about the company's dividend practices. The computational formula and the information content of each ratio is explained below.

Price-earnings ratio (P/E ratio) measures investors' expectations about a company's future earnings. If investors are paying a high price for the stock, this indicates that they expect significant growth in future earnings and the P/E ratio will be high, e.g., in the 30s or higher. If investors will only pay a low price for the stock, they are indicating pessimism about future earnings growth and the P/E ratio will be low, e.g., in single digits.

$$\frac{\text{current market price of common stock}}{\text{diluted earnings per share}}$$

Dividend payout ratio reveals the percentage of the income earned by the common stock that was paid out in common dividends. In other words, it yields the portion of earnings per share that is paid out as dividends.

$$\frac{\text{total cash dividends paid on common stock}}{\text{net income minus preferred dividends}}$$

Dividend yield ratio ratio measures the cash return per share of common stock. (Note that the *total return* on a share of stock would include both the cash dividend plus or minus the change in the market price of the share.)

$$\frac{\text{cash dividend per share of common stock}}{\text{market price per share of common stock}}$$

8. Compute your firm's price-earnings ratio.

   a. price earnings ratio $= \dfrac{\text{current market price of common stock}}{\text{diluted earnings per share}}$

   price earnings ratio $=$ _____ $=$ _____

   ## Note
   The current market price of your firm's common stock can be obtained from the most recent issue of *The Wall Street Journal* (published every weekday and available in most libraries). You will find the stock prices in Section C. Alternatively, the Sunday edition of most local newspapers carry a summary of end-of-the-week corporate stock prices.

   ## On the Internet
   Numerous financial web sites, including many companies, have up-to-date stock quotations. If you need help finding your company's current stock price, go to the Baldwin homepage at **baldwin.swcollege.com**, select "assignments," and utilize the links for Assignment 12.

   b. Based on the Note about P/E ratios, what does your firm's price-earnings ratio tend to indicate about investors' expectations regarding the company's future earnings?

   _____

   _____

   _____

_____

_____

_____

_____

_____

_____

_____

9. Compute your firm's dividend payout ratio.

a. dividend payout ratio = $\dfrac{\text{total cash dividends on common stock}}{\text{net income minus preferred dividends}}$

dividend payout ratio = _____ = _____

b. Assuming the dividend payout ratio you just computed has been fairly constant over recent years, briefly explain what this implies about the company's dividend payment policy.

_____

_____

_____

_____

_____

_____

_____

10. Compute your firm's dividend yield ratio.

a. dividend yield ratio = $\dfrac{\text{cash dividend per share of common stock}}{\text{current market price per share of common stock}}$

dividend yield ratio = _____ = _____

b. Assuming the dividend yield ratio you just computed has been fairly constant over recent years, briefly explain what this reveals about the cash return an owner receives on his/her investment each year. Do you believe this is a satisfactory return on a stockholder's investment? What other source of return (besides dividends) do stockholders earn on their investment?

_____

_____

_____

_____

_____

_____

_____

_____

_____

_____

_____

11. Your third memo is based on your company's investing (long-term assets) and financing (debt and equity) activities.

Guide for Memo No. 3

a. What can you conclude about your company's investing policies? Discuss, using ratios when appropriate.

b. What can you conclude about your company's financing activities? Discuss, using ratios when appropriate.

c. What new insights do you have relative to your assessment of your company? Discuss whether or not you are now more favorably impressed with your company.

Reading 12
Don't Be Fooled By Stock-Split Mania

Reprinted with permission of AOL Time Warner.

By Herb Greenberg
Senior columnist for TheStreet.com.

This split thing is getting way out of hand. Not long ago, in response to a reader who wanted to know if there was any Internet site that predicted stock splits, I wrote, "Not that I know of." Goes to show what I don't know. I got bombarded by readers giving me the name of a Website that claims to know which companies will be next to split their stocks. The site— which I won't identify, on moral grounds— touts trading splits as "very profitable." It goes on to say: "We have a large, power-packed group of stocks we feel will announce splits very soon. Wouldn't you relish the idea of owning the stock before the split announcement?"

Oh, please! When the possibility of a split becomes the chief reason to buy a stock—so much so that investors wear beepers to alert them to splits—we're all in trouble. Splits, after all, began as a Wall Street gimmick to help individual investors avoid a penalty that brokers used to charge for "odd lot" purchases (fewer than 100 shares of a given stock). Companies like it when retail investors buy their stock, because individuals are generally considered more loyal than institutions, but the higher a company's stock price rises, the fewer individuals there are who can afford to buy a 100-share block. "American management discovered long ago that the average individual investor likes to buy stocks that trade at $40 per share," says veteran market pundit Bob Stovall, of Stovall/Twenty First Advisers. Hence, the urge to split.

But today the so-called "odd-lot differential" has disappeared, and individuals have become just as fickle as institutions. So stock splits are now often little more than hocus-pocus to trick unsophisticated investors into thinking they're getting a bargain when they really aren't—the Wall Street equivalent of pricing something at $19.99 instead of $20. In the most common of all splits, a two for one, one share at $50 becomes two shares at $25. Yet you're no wealthier than you were. The company's capitalization is no different than it was. Technically, nothing has changed except the perception that the stock has suddenly become cheap and affordable.

That perception, however, is very strong. Splits have become a "retail phenomenon," says Bill Meehan, chief market strategist at Cantor Fitzgerald. The number of New York Stock Exchange splits rose by 41%, to 235, between 1996 and 1997 and stayed at roughly the same volume in 1998. Last year, according to S&P, some companies even split their stocks twice. (Sorry, but nobody keeps statistics of Nasdaq splits, which is where much of the most questionable action has taken place, thanks to the insanity over Internet stocks.)

"People have always loved splits," says Joe Tigue, managing editor of Standard & Poor's *The Outlook* newsletter. Tigue says you really can predict stock splits, which is why his 80-year-old publication gets frequent requests to reprint its list of split candidates. "If a company has a history of splitting, and the price is where it was when the last split occurred, chances are it'll split again," he says.

In the past, in fact, stocks that split tended to go higher, according to S&P—but not because of the split: They went up because earnings were rising. (There was a time, in fact, when splits were always followed by a boost in a company's quarterly dividend.) "Earnings can be faked, they can be transient," Stovall says. "But dividends reflect real value." Without earnings and dividends, he adds, "all you're doing is fanning the speculative fires."

Which is what seems to be going on much of the time in today's split-crazy market. Stocks that are splitting often have no earnings momentum or even any earnings at all—Internet stocks being notable examples. And dividend increases have become very rare.

The final reason this split

thing is getting out of control: While splits remain a hit with small investors, they've also become a favorite of the day-trading/momentum crowd, which bounces from one hot stock to another in search of anything that will produce a trade. The trend hasn't gone unnoticed by corporate executives, who are under pressure to manage the performance of their stocks. Notice that when Amazon.com's stock started to swoon back in November, the company announced a split. Never mind that it isn't expected to post a profit for another year or two. Amazon said the reason for the split was to increase liquidity by boosting the number of shares outstanding. And Amazon's stock immediately reversed itself and within weeks added more than 100 points as it crossed the $300 mark.

The stock-split mania isn't going to end anytime soon. If you find you're starting to believe the hype, ask yourself two questions: Why does Berkshire Hathaway trade above $60,000 per share, and why has it never split? The answer: Because Warren Buffett believes that over the long term, tricks don't necessarily make the best trade.

Fortune
February 1, 1999
Pages 154 and 156

Questions for Consideration

1. How does a stock split affect shareholders and why would they want the company to increase its dividend at the same time as it announces a stock split?

2. Based on what you know about a stock split, what do you think a reverse stock split is and why would a company use one?

Assignment 13
Segment Information

Name of your company _____

Most large publicly-traded companies have operations in more than one line of
business, or operate in various geographic areas, or have different parts of the
business subject to differing levels of regulation. The purpose of this assignment
is to understand the component parts (segments) of your company's operations.
Are some segments growing more rapidly than others? Which are generating most
of the company's sales and profits?

To help financial statement users make better judgments about the company as a
whole, GAAP require that companies split out certain specific information by
segment. To meet these disclosure requirements, firms usually organize their
financial results into two, three, or four segments. Seldom does a company report
more than five segments. Usually this information is reported near the end of the
notes section. In this assignment you will focus primarily on segment revenues,
segment assets, and segment profit.

> ## Note
> Some firms report that they operate as a single segment. If this is
> the situation for your firm, you will not be able to complete this
> assignment. Ask your professor if he/she would like you to use a
> different company for this part of the **FRP**.

Completing the Assignment

1. Find and read your firm's segment information in the notes to the financial
   statements. (It's usually one of the last notes.) What is the basis your firm has
   chosen upon which to report segments? Mark one below.

   _____ Products or services

   _____ Geography

   _____ Regulatory environment

   _____ Type of customer

   _____ Other

2. What are the names of your firm's segments and what are the primary types of products that are sold in each? Complete the table below.

Segment Name	Types of Products Sold
a.	
b.	
c.	
d.	
e.	
f.	

3. To determine whether management is "growing" one or more of the segments faster than the others, complete the following table by using the data provided in the notes. Divide (1) the segment's total expenditures for long-term assets by (2) the segment's total assets. Do this for each segment for up to three years.

Total expenditures for long-term assets ÷ total assets

Segment Name	Most Recent Year	Next Most Recent Year	Second Most Recent Year
a. _____	_____ %	_____ %	_____ %
b. _____	_____ %	_____ %	_____ %
c. _____	_____ %	_____ %	_____ %
d. _____	_____ %	_____ %	_____ %
e. _____	_____ %	_____ %	_____ %
f. _____	_____ %	_____ %	_____ %

4. Does your analysis in No. 3. indicate that management is "growing" one or more segments more rapidly than the others? Why might this be? Discuss.

_____

_____

_____

_____

_____

5. Complete the table of segment information below. List the segment profit, segment assets, and return on segment assets (of each segment) for the most recent year and two prior years. List the most recent year's information first. Divide column A by column B to obtain the return on segment assets.

Segment Names	Year	A ÷ Segment Profit	B = Segment Assets	Return on Segment Assets
a. _____	___	_____	_____	_____
	___	_____	_____	_____
	___	_____	_____	_____
b. _____	___	_____	_____	_____
	___	_____	_____	_____
	___	_____	_____	_____
c. _____	___	_____	_____	_____
	___	_____	_____	_____
	___	_____	_____	_____
d. _____	___	_____	_____	_____
	___	_____	_____	_____
	___	_____	_____	_____
e. _____	___	_____	_____	_____
	___	_____	_____	_____
	___	_____	_____	_____
f. _____	___	_____	_____	_____
	___	_____	_____	_____
	___	_____	_____	_____

6. Discuss the results of your segment profitability analysis and include the following.

▸ What trends do you observe?

▸ Are some segments performing better than others?

▸ What segment-related questions would you ask of management if you had the opportunity?

▸ Might overall profitability be enhanced by reallocating assets to some segments and away from others?

▸ Does management address "segment strategies" in the Management Discussion and Analysis section of the Annual Report? What do they say? Discuss and explain.

Note

To better understand profit results, analysts often split return on assets into two component parts: profit margin and asset turnover.

1. The *profit margin* reveals the number of pennies out of each sales dollar that a company retains (as profit) after paying all of its expenses.

$$\text{segment profit margin} = \frac{\text{segment profit}}{\text{total segment revenues}}$$

2. *Asset turnover* reveals how many times during the accounting period that those pennies were earned.

$$\text{segment asset turnover} = \frac{\text{total segment revenues}}{\text{segment assets}}$$

Ideally, companies would prefer to have high profit margin **and** high asset turnover. In reality, companies vary widely in their combinations of margin and turnover. Similarly, segments can vary widely in their margins and turnover. A segment's profit margin multiplied by its asset turnover equals the return on segment assets for that segment.

return on segment assets = segment profit margin × segment asset turnover

7. To understand more about how your company's segment profits are generated, compute the profit margin, asset turnover, and return on segment assets for each of your firm's segments. Use the formulas from the Note above for your computations of each segment's profit margin, asset turnover, and return on segment assets.

Segment Name	Segment Profit Margin $\dfrac{\text{segment profit}}{\text{total segment revenues}}$	×	Segment Asset Turnover $\dfrac{\text{total segment revenues}}{\text{segment assets}}$	=	Return on Segment Assets
a. _____	_____		_____		_____
b. _____	_____		_____		_____
c. _____	_____		_____		_____
d. _____	_____		_____		_____
e. _____	_____		_____		_____
f. _____	_____		_____		_____

8. Discuss the comparative profit margins and asset turnover that you computed for your company's segments. Do they differ markedly or they all about the same? If there are significant differences, is there anything about the nature of the various products in the different segments that would tend to explain the differences you found? Discuss.

_____

_____

_____

_____

_____

_____

_____

_____

_____

_____

_____

_____

_____

_____

_____

_____

_____

_____

_____

_____

_____

_____

_____

_____

_____

_____

_____

Reading 13
Accounting for Differences

By Rose Marie L. Bukics
CPA, professor of economics and business at Lafayette College
Marge O-Reilly-Allen
CPA, assistant professor of acounting at Rider University
Chris Schnittker
controller at Global Sports Inc.

If international accounting standards are here to stay, what do they mean?

True or false: Because you're involved with a U.S. corporation, international accounting standards (IAS), as promulgated by the International Accounting Standards Committee (IASC), have no impact on your current work environment.

True or false: U.S. GAAP is the only acceptable accounting standard used in the global marketplace.

True or false: No corporation in the United States prepares financial statements using IAS standards.

True or false: Companies aren't permitted to use international accounting standards when listing on the London, Zurich, Frankfurt or Hong Kong stock exchanges.

If you answered true to any of these I questions, read this article and its sidebar carefully. While it isn't an exhaustive explanation of financial reporting under IAS, it highlights the differences that may affect a financial executive's information needs. Be aware of these differences and their potential impact on the comparability and reliability of financial information published in the global marketplace.

Heads Up

Although some financial executives may feel removed from the international markets, in reality all businesses operate in the global marketplace. Whether your firm is a multinational corporation or you're the CFO of a small business looking to expand internationally, you must be aware of recent changes in the international accounting arena. International accounting standards have made significant inroads, and the growing influence of the IASC is a serious consideration. You need to recognize that international accounting standards represent an alternative approach acceptable in many countries and on many stock exchanges. They're here to stay.

Consider the following events that have occured within the past four years:

✦ The European Union (EU) has concluded that IAS are the preferred option for the future development of accounting in EU countries.

✦ The finance ministers and central bank governors of the G7 countries recently expressed support for IAS as a means to attaining greater transparency and openness in the world financial markets.

✦ The World Trade Organization has announced its support for the work of the IASC.

✦ The International Organization of Securities Committees (IOSCO) agreed to consider international accounting standards for endorsement of cross border filings if the IASC would prepare a set of core standards. The IASC recently completed the core standards project; the results are under IOSCO review.

✦ The SEC has changed its rules to align its non-financial disclosure requirements with those issued by the IASC. It's also currently reviewing the core standards issued by the IASC.

✦ France and Germany recently passed legislation allowing both foreign and domestic companies to use IAS, rather than home country accounting principles, in the preparation of consolidated financial statements. Other EU countries, such as Italy and Belgium, have similar laws pending.

✦ Australia has mandated that IAS become the country's accounting standard.

✦ IASC 33, *Earnings Per Share*, has been judged by some professionals to be equivalent to FASB 128, and both boards have other similar projects on their current agendas (for example, the use of present value in accounting measurements).

The 39 Steps

To date, the IASC has issued 39 standards, used by more than 660 companies in 69 countries and accepted by 39 of the world's stock exchanges. Though some of the companies and countries are small, some large multinationals also use IASC standards. For example, Nestle, Bayer, Renault, Saint Gobain, Porsche, Olivetti, Asea Brown Boveri and Microsoft (yes, even Microsoft) currently report financial information under IASC guidelines. While the SEC doesn't currently accept statements prepared under IAS guidelines for any U.S. stock exchange without a reconciliation to U.S.-based GAAP, it's currently reviewing the core standards completed by the IASC and submitted to IOSCO. However, many major stock exchanges – including London, Tokyo, Hong Kong, Paris, Frankfurt, Rome, Brussels, Easdaq, Luxembourg and Oslo – permit IAS prepared statements.

IASC core standards impact all aspects of financial statement reporting. An examination of their titles suggests many of the topics covered under FASB and APB pronouncements are the same as those covered by the IASC pronouncements.

However, it's important to note that while many of the topics are the same, not all of the results are. Such differences can arise because FASB pronouncements often contain more guidance for the user than is provided under IAS, or because several IAS still allow for alternative approaches (though now most of the pronouncements specify a benchmark or preferred treatment vs. that of an allowed but alternative treatment). When differences exist – and there's some disagreement among both practitioners and scholars as to the significance of those differences – evaluate the results on a case by case basis.

Sidebar

Apples to Apples

Here are some areas to consider when assessing financial results under international accounting standards.

Balance Sheet

The major financial reporting issues governing balance sheet presentation, if prepared under IAS 1 (revised in 1997 and effective for statements issued after July 1, 1998), are classification and valuation of assets.

If a financial executive is interested in assessing liquidity in a company using IAS, there are differences to note in account classification. While IAS statements clearly report non-current assets before current assets, the time frame used for classification of current vs. non-current may not be as readily apparent. Although typically 12 months, IAS mandate that inventory, accounts receivable, accounts payable and other accruals for operating costs be classified as current whether or not they're expected to impact cash within 12 months.

And while IAS 1 provides guidelines on balance sheet preparation and presentation, it doesn't provide guidance on the valuation of balance sheet accounts. Those standards are found in a variety of IAS pronouncements. Although some of the balance sheet items are valued in a manner similar to those prescribed by U.S. GAAP, differences may arise in key areas such as plant and equipment, inventory and investments.

As to the other side of the balance sheet, the IASC has issued little guidance on equity components to date. It's important to note, however, that any change in the valuation of plant and equipment, intangibles or long-term investments results in a revaluation reserve that appears in the equity section of the balance sheet.

Income Statement

IAS 1 also governs the overall preparation and presentation of the income statement. While the presentation of income statement items is similar under both international and U.S. standards, the results may not be comparable because of different accounting treatments in determining the reported amounts. Key areas where differences might occur are discontinued operations, restructuring charges, extraordinary items, research and development, accounting changes (in principal, estimate or errors) and employee benefits. Such differences may occur either because IAS may allow alternative treatments for such events, or because the IAS lacks specific guidance on measurement criteria, therefore allowing companies some latitude in determining results.

Statement of Cash Flows

For financial statements prepared under IAS, the cash flow statement is governed by IAS 7, issued in 1977 and revised in 1992. The standard for presenting cash flow information corresponds closely to the U.S. standard (SFAS 95), with a few minor classification exceptions. Under IAS 7, companies may present interest expense as a financing activity rather than as an operating activity as classified under SFAS 95. Also, under IAS 7, companies may choose to report interest and dividend income from investments as investing activities or operating activities, rather than as operating activities required under SFAS 95.

Some of these balance sheet classification issues may generate comparability problems in the cash flow statement, too, For example, cash or bank overdrafts, typically reclassified to the liability side of the balance sheet for reporting under U.S. GAAP, can be shown as offsets to cash and cash equivalents under IAS 7, provided they result from the company's normal cash management strategies. This contradiction results in a different presentation of changes in cash and financing activity on the statement of cash flows.

It's also important to note that U.S. GAAP and the IAS differ in their approach to complex transactions that could have multiple classifications in the cash flows statement. While U.S. GAAP requires that the most significant part of the transaction determine how it's classified on the cash flow statement, IAS allow such transactions to be reported in various sections of the cash flow statement. This may make analyzing the cash flow effects of a particular transaction an elusive game of hide-and-seek.

Financial Executive
Mar/Apr 2000
Pages 36 – 38

Questions for Consideration

1. Since international standards are used in many countries and accepted by many stock exchanges, do you think that the FASB and SEC refusal to accept international standards puts U.S. investors at a disadvantage in the capital markets?

2. List two differences between balance sheets and income statements as prepared under U.S. and international accounting standards. How could an investor be made aware of these differences?

Assignment 14
The Cash Flow Statement

Name of your company _____

The purpose of this assignment is to understand the information presented on your company's cash flow statement. This financial statement is the only one that is *not* based on accrual accounting. It is a simple report of how much cash flowed into the company and how much cash flowed out. You will compare and contrast your company's cash flows from operating, financing, and investing activities.

Completing the Assignment

1. Indicate with a check mark below whether your firm's cash flow statement was prepared using the direct approach or the indirect approach.

    a. _____ *Direct approach.* If the first line under Operating Activities reads "Cash received from customers," or something similar, the direct approach is being used.

    b. _____ *Indirect approach.* If the first line under Operating Activities reads "Net income," or something similar, the indirect approach is being used.

2. Does the net "change in cash" (sometimes labeled change in cash and cash equivalents) as reported on the cash flow statement match the change in cash balance reported on the comparative balance sheets for the most recent two year period? If no, indicate the amount of change.

    _____ Yes

    _____ No $_____ Amount of change

> **Note**
> The linkage of an item on one financial statement to an item reported on a different financial statement is referred to as *financial statement articulation.*

---

3. Unless a firm issued significant amounts of equity or debt, e.g., stocks or bonds, during a year, operating activities should be the largest source of cash. If operating activities aren't generating a significant amount of cash from year to year, the firm may be headed for trouble. A company that is regularly generating cash from investing activities also may be headed for trouble, i.e., the company may be selling off assets to pay its bills.

a. Prepare a summary of your firm's cash flows. There should be three years of data on the statement of cash flows. There may be additional years summarized in the Financial Highlights section. Report as many years as you can, but not more than six, in millions of dollars.

	Most Recent Year	Prior Years (label each column below)				
Category	_____	_____	_____	_____	_____	_____
Operating activities	_____	_____	_____	_____	_____	_____
Investing activities	_____	_____	_____	_____	_____	_____
Financing activities	_____	_____	_____	_____	_____	_____
Net change in cash during year	_____	_____	_____	_____	_____	_____

b. What do you conclude from the information above? Does the company appear to be generating a healthy cash flow from operations over the years or is it depending on cash from other sources to pay its bills? Discuss.

If cash from operations is often negative, it is a particularly bad sign. It means that every day when the company opens for business some of its cash "leaks out."

_____

_____

_____

_____

_____

_____

_____

_____

_____

_____

_____

_____

_____

_____

_____

_____

_____

_____

_____

_____

_____

_____

4. Usually, a company's operating activities and financing activities supply cash for investing activities.   Examine your company's investing activities.

   a. Determine the amounts of cash and fill in the blanks below in millions of dollars.

	Most Recent Year	Prior Years (label each column below)				
	____	____	____	____	____	____
1) Cash generated (used) by operating activities **plus** financing activities	____	____	____	____	____	____
2) Cash generated (used) by investing activities	____	____	____	____	____	____

   3) Is the cash provided by operating activities and financing activities together roughly equal to the amount of cash consumed by investing activities in each year? Answer "yes" or "no" for each year. (More than one "no" may indicate that further inquiry into cash flow is necessary.)

____	____	____	____	____	____

   b. Summarize your findings regarding 4.a. In general, is the *usual* situation occurring for your firm during the years studied? Are cash outflows from investing activities being adequately covered by cash inflows from operating activities and financing activities? Discuss.

_____

_____

_____

_____

_____

_____

_____

_____

_____

_____

_____

Note

Three ratios often are computed to assess the cash flow results of a firm.

Cash-based return on assets ratio is the cash-based equivalent of the accrual-based return on assets. In each case, the intent is to compare the results of operations to the amount of assets used to generate that result.

$$\frac{\text{net cash flow from operating activities}}{\text{average total assets}^*}$$

Cash flows to current maturities of long-term debt ratio is a coverage ratio which measures the number of times that this year's current maturities of long-term debt could have been repaid from cash generated by this year's operating activities.

$$\frac{\text{net cash flow from operating activities}}{\text{current maturities of long} \cdot \text{term debt}}$$

Cash used by investing activities to long-term assets ratio measures the rate at which long-term assets are being replaced. A high ratio indicates that the firm is not merely replacing assets but is growing. A low rate may indicate that the company is failing to replace long-term assets on a timely basis and faces a risk of obsolescence.

$$\frac{\text{cash used by investing activities}}{\text{average long} \cdot \text{term assets}^*}$$

* beginning total (long · term) assets + ending total (long · term assets

2

---

5. Compute each of the ratios below for the most recent year for your firm.

    a.   cash based return on assets $=\dfrac{\text{net cash flow from operating activities}}{\text{average total assets}}$

    cash based return on assets $=$ _____ $=$ _____

    b. $\begin{pmatrix} \text{cash flows to current maturities} \\ \text{of long}\cdot\text{term debt} \end{pmatrix} = \dfrac{\text{net cash flow from operating activities}}{\text{current maturities of long}\cdot\text{term debt}}$

    $\begin{pmatrix} \text{cash flows to current maturities} \\ \text{of long}\cdot\text{term debt} \end{pmatrix} =$ _____ $=$ _____

    c. $\begin{pmatrix} \text{cash used by investing activities} \\ \text{to long}\cdot\text{term debt} \end{pmatrix} = \dfrac{\text{cash used by investing activities}}{\text{average long}\cdot\text{term assets}}$

    $\begin{pmatrix} \text{cash used by investing activities} \\ \text{to long}\cdot\text{term debt} \end{pmatrix} =$ _____ $=$ _____

6. To give perspective to the ratios computed above, check with five classmates to compare the value of the ratios for their firms to yours. Record the information below.

Alternative

As an alternative to comparing your company's values with those of your classmates' companies, you may want to compare with the companies you used in No. 3.e. of Assignment 5.

Check with your professor to make sure this option is acceptable.

	Your Firm	COMPARATIVE FIRMS				
		Firm 1	Firm 2	Firm 3	Firm 4	Firm 5
a. Cash-based return on assets	____	____	____	____	____	____
b. Cash flows to current maturities of long-term debt	____	____	____	____	____	____
c. Cash used by investing activities to long-term debt	____	____	____	____	____	____

7. How do your firm's cash-based ratios correlate to those of your comparative firms? Do some appear high? Some low? All about the same? Be specific.

    Is there anything about your firm, its industry, or your comparative companies or industries that would tend to explain the differences between your company's ratios and those of other firms? Discuss.

8. Did your firm report any significant *noncash* financing and investing activities (often called direct exchanges) for its most recent year? For example, issuing common stock (financing activity) to acquire land (investment activity) is normally considered a significant noncash financing and investing activity.

   Hint: These usually are found at the bottom of the statement of cash flows or in a separate schedule that accompanies the statement of cash flows.

   a. If yes, describe these transactions below. If no, write "none."

   _____

   _____

   _____

   _____

   _____

   _____

   _____

   _____

   _____

   _____

   _____

   _____

   b. For each item listed in 8.a. explain how the transaction affected your firm's balance sheet.

   _____

   _____

   _____

   _____

   _____

   _____

   _____

   _____

   _____

   _____

   _____

   _____

   _____

9. Now that you have studied your company's segment and cash flow information, you have all the information needed to complete your analysis of your company.

Guide for Memo No. 4

a. Did you find the segment disclosures sufficient for you to gain a better understanding of your company? Are the reported segments consistent with what you thought your company would have as segments? Explain.

b. Over the three years of cash flow information found in your company's reported Cash Flow Statement, has your company's cash position improved, weakened, or remained about the same? Explain.

c. Using all that you now know about your company, analyze its overall financial health, using ratios where appropriate, and make a recommendation about including your company in an equity portfolio. Explain why you would or would not include it.

Reading 14
Fading Beauty

By Debra Sparks in New York

Revlon is drowning in red ink, the stock is in a slump, and Perelman's options are limited.

Ronald O. Perelman has achieved almost cultlike status on Wall Street. A self-made billionaire, Perelman has long bought and sold companies with illustrious brand names like Marvel Entertainment, Coleman, Consolidated Cigar, and Revlon Consumer Products. Adding to Perelman's celeb status, Revlon recently lured the international country-pop star Shania Twain as one of its spokespersons. But even in its newest TV ads, this red-lipsticked diva, dressed in skimpy black sequined dress and top hat, can't sing and dance Revlon out of its current state of the blues.

Revlon, one of the leading cosmetic companies, is 83% owned by Perelman through his company McAndrews & Forbes Holdings Inc. But Revlon's stock is acting anything but glamorous these days: Over the past year it has slumped from $32^1/_4$ to $9^{15}/_{16}$. Net income of $13 million in the third quarter last year has turned into a loss of $165 million in this year's third quarter. Revlon has generated positive cash flow from operations in only three of the last 11 quarters. Meanwhile debt to total capitalization is 200%, and this year's cash flow from operations has been insufficient to pay off its steadily rising interest expense. No wonder some analysts predict such dire possibilities as default, even bankruptcy.

Revlon's major operational problems stem from an assault on Revlon's core business from such deep-pocketed rivals as Johnson & Johnson's Neutrogena division and Procter & Gamble's Oil of Olay. Revlon blames its current malaise on drugstores slashing their inventory from 11 months to two months, due to sharp industry consolidation. As a result, Revlon expects a 24% reduction in sales in the last half of 1999. All this has taken its toll. Three top execs recently resigned, including CEO George Fellows. On Dec. 5, Jeffrey Nugent, formerly worldwide president of Neutrogena Inc., will replace him. Revlon has also announced the sale of its Latin American and professional products divisions, which the company hopes will fetch $500 million to be used to pay down debt.

Yet there could be more bad news. "I think it's a real possibility that Revlon files for bankruptcy within the next 12 months," says Al Alaimo, a high-yield analyst with Bank of America Securities in New York. "The company's operations appear to be a mess. They have too much leverage and they're bleeding cash."

Howard Gittis, vice-chairman of McAndrews & Forbes, would not comment on Revlon's financial future. But he says the likelihood of Revlon's operating company going bankrupt "is absurd."

Over the years, Perelman has displayed his ability to get out of financial scrapes. Indeed, some consider him a financial wizard who constructs complicated organizational structures. Perelman entities like Marvel Entertainment and Coleman had similar strategies: A majority of the operating company is owned by Perelman through a series of holding companies. Typically, he gets his personal money off the table quickly while still maintaining control, leaving little downside risk for himself. In many cases, he obtains liquidity by issuing high-yield debt through shell holding companies.

Marvel Mess

But this high-yield debt can get bondholders in trouble. That's because some of the bonds are collateralized by Perelman's own stock instead of the assets of the company. Under that arrangement, Perelman can make it difficult for investors to get the collateral in a bankruptcy. In 1997 when Marvel went bankrupt, Perelman forced some of Marvel's bondholders to go to court to get the collateral. It was messy.

That could be the fate of some Revlon bondholders. In the same year as Marvel bondholders were duking it out in court, Perelman issued $770 million of high-yield Revlon bonds under similar arrangements. These bonds are already deeply discounted, trading at 25 cents on the dollar. "They are some of the riskiest bonds in the high-yield market," says Ike Michaels, a distressed securities analyst with The Weston Group in New York.

And now some analysts are beginning to wonder whether these bonds are headed for default. They are backed by collateral consisting of Perelman's 20 million unregistered shares of Revlon's operating company. To pay back the bondholders, Perelman's stock must be at $38^1/_2$—vs. its current $9^{15}/_{16}$. Gittis will not comment on what Revlon will do when the bonds mature, or whether they will default.

Holding the Bag?

There may still be time to resuscitate the ailing operating company and boost its stock price, since the bonds don't come due until March, 2001. But some think it's already a lost cause. "This stock has as much a chance of reaching $38 as I have of getting pregnant," says Andrew Shore, an analyst with PaineWebber Inc. in New York.

Alaimo thinks Perelman will default on the holding company bonds and that it "could lead to another battle between ... bondholders and Perelman," as in the case with Marvel. Investors took huge losses when the price of the bonds and stock collapsed. Ultimately a court ruled in favor of the bondholders, but the victory was costly in terms of legal fees.

Why did Marvel bondholders have to sue to get the collateral they were owed? "There was no mechanism ... to handle the turnover of the collateral," says Gittis. The bonds were structured to make it as difficult as possible for bondholders to get their collateral. It may come as a nasty little surprise to Revlon bondholders that Revlon paper is similarly structured.

Revlon's holding company, of course, could refinance the bonds. But the value of the collateral, now worth $200 million, is insufficient to raise the $770 million needed to repay bondholders. One of the few hopes for the company is the impending asset sales. But Shore doubts Revlon will raise $500 million. "Why pay $500 million if you know this company is in desperate need of money and you know you could get it for less?"

If Shore is right, this could put Revlon's bondholders in the same position as the Marvel bondholders. It may take more than Spider-Man to save them from the complicated web Perelman has spun.

Business Week
December 13, 1999
Pages 156 and 158

Questions for Consideration

1. The article states that bondholders may suffer huge losses because Revlon's cash position is so weak. If you were a Revlon *shareholder*, what would your reaction be to Revlon's cash position?

2. Using the Internet, review Revlon's Statement of Cash Flows. What do the net operating, investing and financing cash flows indicate about Revlon's cash activities and its ability to recover from its current cash flow dilemma?

Assignment 15
Capstone Project

The purpose of this assignment is to integrate the information you have obtained about your company (or companies) and industry into a coordinated report. The report is to be typed and have a professional appearance. You should assume that your first post-college employer has asked you to research the firm you've been working on during this course. He/she may be considering your firm as a potential supplier, customer, competitor, or acquisition candidate. Your employer may even be secretly entertaining an offer of employment from this firm. Under any of these circumstances, you will want to present your employer with a carefully-researched, thoughtfully-written, and professionally-presented document.

Completing The Assignment

In general, unless modified by your professor, you have great flexibility in completing this assignment. For example, you may choose any organization structure for this report that you believe best captures and presents the necessary information. You should be creative and complete in your analyses and presentation. Generally, your report is to be based on the assignments you have completed during this course as part of the **Financial Reporting Project** (**FRP**). In some cases, however, you will want to include additional information or additional creative analysis that is especially important to understanding the financial health and status of your firm (or firms) and industry. Where appropriate, you should prepare charts or graphs to illustrate the facts you present.

Keep in mind that your employer may put your report to a variety of uses. For example:

- If your assigned firm is a prospective supplier, your employer would want to assess its long-run stability and its continuing ability to provide quality goods at reasonable prices.

- If your assigned firm is a potential customer, your employer will be concerned with its ability to meet its short-term obligations as they become due.

- If your assigned firm is a candidate for investment, your employer will want to understand its long-term financial structure, cost structure, and profit structure.

Your report should be flexible so that it can be used in any of these ways. Regardless of the format you use, your report must include a summary section that states your overall assessment of the financial health and status of your firm. For example, is it strong, weak, improving, or deteriorating? Would you make a short-term loan to this firm? Would you make a long-term loan to this firm? Would you buy stock or invest your career with this company? Discuss why or why not.

1. **Suggested Outline** – If you are unsure how to organize your report you might consider the following outline. It follows the assignment structure of the **FRP**.

   Important: *Be sure to check with your professor to determine if he/she has specific guidelines regarding the organization of your report.*

   a. Overview of the Industry

   b. Basic Company Information

   c. The Company's Economic, Social, Legal and Political Environment

   d. Overview of the Annual Report, SEC 10-K and Proxy Statement

   e. The Company's Independent Auditor

   f. The Income Statement

   g. Current Assets and Current Liabilities

   h. Long-term Assets and Long-term Liabilities

   i. Stockholders' Equity

   j. Segment Information

   k. The Cash Flow Statement

   l. Summary Statement on Financial Health and Status of the Company

   If you use this suggested outline, be careful that you don't merely make lists of the information that you collected on the assignment sheets of the **FRP**. The outline format of the assignments is very efficient for recording the data you found for your company, but it won't be very helpful to your employer. Remember, your employer hasn't read the articles or consulted the references that you have. You are expected to provide greater background, detail, analysis and commentary than what appears in your completed assignments.

2. **Due Date(s)** – To be announced by your professor.

3. **Annual Report**, **SEC 10-K**, and **Proxy Statement** – If you have not already done so, provide each of these documents to your professor when you turn in your report.

Note

If you are part of a team in which each member is researching a different firm, avoid the temptation to write a separate report for each company and staple the reports together. Instead, this report should be an *integrated* report in which the firms are compared, contrasted, and summarized in each section.

Your report must focus on comparisons and contrasts among the firms and on an integrated assessment of the overall industry situation. You are expected to provide greater background, detail, and analysis than what appears in your individual completed assignments.

Appendix
Listing of Synonyms

One of the perplexing aspects of learning accounting is that there is so much variation in terminology. Often, two or more terms mean exactly (or very nearly) the same thing. If you don't recognize a particular term, look it up here. You may have already learned the concept or principle under a similar or different name.

Accounting Term

Alternative Accounting Terms

A

Accounting Term	Alternative Accounting Terms
Acid-Test Ratio	Quick Ratio
Accounting Equation	Basic Accounting Equation; Balance Sheet Equation
Accounting Rate of Return	Simple Rate of Return
Allowance for Bad Debts	Allowance for Doubtful Accounts; Allowance for Uncollectible Accounts
Allowance for Doubtful Accounts	see Allowance for Bad Debts
Allowance for Uncollectible Accounts	see Allowance for Bad Debts
Annuity	Ordinary Annuity
Asset	Unexpired Cost

B

Accounting Term	Alternative Accounting Terms
Bad Debts Expense	Uncollectible Accounts Expense
Balance Sheet	Statement of Financial Position; Statement of Financial Condition
Balance Sheet Equation	Accounting Equation; Basic Accounting Equation
Basic Accounting Equation	Accounting Equation; Balance Sheet Equation
Basket Purchase	Lump-sum Purchase (or acquisition); Joint Purchase; Group Purchase
Bearer Bond	Coupon Bond
Book of Original Entry	Journal; General Journal
Book Value	Carrying Value
Burden	Factory Burden; Overhead; Manufacturing Overhead
Business Entity Concept	Entity Concept; Separate Entity Concept

C

Accounting Term	Alternative Accounting Terms
Capital Stock	generic term for either common or preferred stock
Carrying Value	Book Value
Cash Discount	either a Sales Discount or Purchase Discount, depending on the circumstances
Cash Value	Fair Value; Fair Market Value; Market Value
Cash Equivalent Value	same as Cash Value
Charge an account	Debit an Account
Closely Held Corporation	Nonpublic Corporation
Common Stock	Capital Stock
Constant-Dollar Accounting	Price-Level Accounting; GPL Accounting
Contract (Interest) Rate	Stated Rate; Coupon Rate; Nominal Rate; Face Rate
Continuity Principle	Going Concern Principle
Contributed Capital	Paid-In Capital

Contribution Approach to Pricing	Variable Approach to Pricing
Coupon Bond	Bearer Bond
Coupon (Interest) Rate	Stated Rate; Nominal Rate; Face Rate; Contract Rate
Current Cost Accounting	Current Value Accounting
Current Ratio	Working Capital Ratio
Current Value Accounting	Current Cost Accounting

D

Debenture Bond	Unsecured Bond
Differential Cost	Incremental Cost
Direct Costing	Variable Costing
Direct Labor Efficiency Variance	Labor Efficiency Variance; Labor Usage Variance; Direct Labor Usage Variance
Direct Labor Price Variance	see Direct Labor Rate Variance
Direct Labor Rate Variance	Labor Price Variance; Direct Labor Price Variance; Labor Rate Variance
Direct Labor Usage Variance	see Direct Labor Efficiency Variance
Direct Materials Quantity Variance	Materials Quantity Variance; Materials Usage Variance; Direct Materials Usage Variance;
Direct Materials Usage Variance	see Direct Materials Quantity Variance

E

Earnings	Income; Profit
Earnings Statement	Income Statement; Profit and Loss Statement
Effective Interest Rate	Market Rate; Yield Rate
Entity Principle (or concept)	Separate Entity Principle (or concept); Business Entity Principle (or concept)
Expense	Expired Cost
Expense and Revenue Summary account	Income Summary account
Expired Cost	Expense

F

Face (Interest) Rate	Stated Rate; Coupon Rate; Nominal Rate; Contract Rate
Face Value (of bonds or notes)	Par Value; Maturity Value; Principal
Factory Burden	Burden; Overhead; Manufacturing Overhead
Fair Market Value	Fair Value; Cash Value; Market Value
Fair Value	Fair Market Value; Cash Value; Market Value
Financial Leverage	Leverage; Trading on the Equity
Fixed Assets	Plant Assets; Productive Assets; Tangible Assets; Property, Plant and Equipment
Freight-In	Transportation-In
*Funds Flow Statement	Statement of Changes in Financial Position; Statement of Changes in Financial Condition

G

Going Concern Principle	Continuity Principle
General Journal	Journal; Book of Original Entry
General Price-Level Accounting	Price-Level Accounting; Constant-Dollar Accounting; GPL Accounting
General Price-Level Gain/Loss	Price-Level Gain/Loss

*An obsolete financial statement that is no longer part of required external financial reporting. In 1987 the Financial Accounting Standards Board (FASB) decided that this statement should be replaced by the *Statement of Cash Flows*.

GPL Accounting	General Price-Level Accounting; Price-Level Accounting; Constant-Dollar Accounting
Gross Margin (on sales)	Gross Profit
Gross Profit (on sales)	Gross Margin
Group Purchase	Basket Purchase; Lump-sum Purchase; Joint Purchase

H

High Yield Bond	Junk Bond; Speculative Grade Bond
Hurdle Rate	Minimum Desired Rate (of return)

I

Income	Earnings; Profit
Income Statement	Earnings Statement; Profit and Loss Statement
Income Summary account	Expense and Revenue Summary account
Incremental Cost	Differential Cost
Internal Rate of Return	Time Adjusted Rate of Return
Inventory	Merchandise Inventory

J

Joint Purchase	Basket Purchase; Lump-sum Purchase; Group Purchase
Journal	General Journal; Book of Original Entry
Junk Bond	High Yield Bond; Speculative Grade Bond

L

Labor Efficiency Variance	see Direct Labor Efficiency Variance
Labor Price Variance	see Direct Labor Rate Variance
Labor Rate Variance	see Direct Labor Rate Variance
Labor Usage Variance	see Direct Labor Efficiency Variance
Leverage	Financial Leverage; Trading on the Equity
Lump-Sum Purchase	Basket Purchase (or acquisition); Joint Purchase; Group Purchase

M

Manufacturing Overhead	Overhead; Burden; Factory Burden
Marketable Securities	Temporary Investments; Short-term Investments
Market (Interest) Rate	Effective Rate; Yield Rate
Market Value	Fair Value; Fair Market Value; Cash Value; Current Value
Materials Quantity Variance	see Direct Materials Quantity Variance
Materials Usage Variance	see Direct Materials Quantity Variance
Maturity Value (of bonds)	Face Value; Principal; Par Value
Merchandise Inventory	Inventory
Minimum Desired Rate (of return)	Hurdle Rate
Monetary Unit Principle	Unit-of-Measure Principle
Mortgage Bond	Secured Bond

N

Net Earnings	Net Income; Net Profit
Net Income	Net Profit; Net Earnings
Net Profit	Net Income; Net Earnings
Nominal Account	Temporary Account
Nominal (Interest) Rate	Stated Rate; Coupon Rate; Face Rate; Contract Rate

Nonpublic Corporation   Closely Held Corporation
Normal Operating Cycle   Operating Cycle

O

Operating Cycle   Normal Operating Cycle
Ordinary Annuity   Annuity
Ordinary Bonds   Term Bonds
Overhead   Manufacturing Overhead; Burden; Factory Burden
Owners' Equity   Shareholders' Equity; Stockholders' Equity

P

Paid-In Capital   Contributed Capital
Partnership Agreement   Partnership Contract; Articles of Co-Partnership
Par Value (of bonds)   Face Value; Principal; Maturity Value
Periodicity Principle   Time-Period Principle
Permanent Account   Real Account
Plant Assets   Fixed Assets; Property, Plant and Equipment;
                                         Productive Assets; Tangible Assets

Preferred Stock   Capital Stock
Price-Level Accounting   Constant-Dollar Accounting; GPL Accounting;
                                         General Price-Level Accounting;

Price-Level Gain/Loss   General Price-Level Gain/Loss
Principal (of bonds)   Face Value; Maturity Value; Par Value
Productive Assets   Plant Assets; Property, Plant and Equipment;
                                         Fixed Assets; Tangible Assets

Profit   Income; Earnings
Profit and Loss Statement   Income Statement; Earnings Statement
Property, Plant and Equipment   Plant Assets; Fixed Assets; Productive Assets;
                                         Tangible Assets

Purchase Discount   Cash Discount

Q

Quick Ratio   Acid-Test Ratio

R

Real Account   Permanent Account

S

Sales Discount   Cash Discount
Secured Bond   Mortgage Bond
Separate Entity Principle   Entity Principle (or concept); Business Entity Principle
Shareholders' Equity   Stockholders' Equity; Owners' Equity
Short-term Investments   Temporary Investments; Marketable Securities
Simple Rate of Return   Accounting Rate of Return
Speculative Grade Bond   Junk Bond; High Yield Bond
Stated (Interest) Rate   Coupon Rate; Face Rate; Nominal Rate; Contract Rate
*Statement of Changes in   Statement of Changes in Financial Condition;
   Financial Position   Funds Flow Statement
*Statement of Changes in   Statement of Changes in Financial Position;
   Financial Condition   Funds Flow Statement

---

*An obsolete financial statement that is no longer part of required external financial reporting. In 1987 the
Financial Accounting Standards Board (FASB) decided that this statement should be replaced by the *Statement of Cash Flows.*

VIA: UP

PRIME-INDCT-GROUP
-SLSB

LOCATION	QTY	ISBN	AUTHOR/TITLE
K-34V-026-10	1	0-324-12580-1	BALDWIN/HOCK THE FIN REPORTING PROJ & READG

WAREHOUSE INSTRUCTIONS

SLA: 7   BOX: Staple

SALES SUPPORT

SHIP TO: MICHAEL FETTERS
BABSON COLL
ACCOUNTING DEPARTMENT
/
BABSON PARK MA 02457

Ship returns to:

THOMSON LEARNING
DISTRIBUTION CENTER
7625 EMPIRE DRIVE
FLORENCE, KY 41042

The enclosed materials are sent to you for your review by
MAUREEN STAUDT 800 8762350X7283

Statement of Financial Position	Balance Sheet; Statement of Financial Condition
Statement of Financial Condition	Balance Sheet; Statement of Financial Position
Stockholders' Equity	Shareholders' Equity; Owners' Equity

T

Tangible Assets	Fixed Assets; Plant Assets; Productive Assets; Property, Plant and Equipment
Tax Avoidance	Tax Planning
Tax Planning	Tax Avoidance
Temporary Account	Nominal Account
Temporary Investments	Short-term Investments; Marketable Securities
Term Bonds	Ordinary Bonds
Time Adjusted Rate of Return	Internal Rate of Return
Time-Period Principle	Periodicity Principle
Trading on the Equity	Leverage; Financial Leverage
Transportation-In	Freight-In

U

Uncollectible Accounts Expense	Bad Debts Expense
Unexpired Cost	Asset
Unit-of-Measure Principle	Monetary Unit Principle
Unsecured Bond	Debenture Bond

V

Variable Approach to Pricing	Contribution Approach to Pricing
Variable Costing	Direct Costing

W

Working Capital Ratio	Current Ratio

Y

Yield (Interest) Rate	Market Rate; Effective Rate